ABT

6/02

Ancient Egypt

Ancient Egypt

and The Middle East

Robert Morkot

Dorling Kindersley

London, New York, Sydney, Delhi, Paris, Munich, and Johannesburg

Publisher: Sean Moore
Editorial Director: Chuck Wills
Project Editor: Barbara Minton
Art Director: Dirk Kaufman
Production Director: David Proffit

Ancient Egypt and the Middle East
0-7894-7833-1

First US edition 2001
Published in the US by
DK Publishing, Inc.
95 Madison Avenue
New York, New York 10016

First published 2001 by
BBC Worldwide Ltd.
Woodlands, 80 Wood Lane,
London W12 0TT

Produced for BBC Worldwide by
Toucan Books, Ltd. London

Cover photograph: Robert Harding/Walter Rawlings

Printed and bound in France by Imprinerie Pollina s.a.
N 80762-C

Color separations by Imprinerie Pollina s.a.

PICTURE CREDITS:
Page 2 Sonia Halliday. 6 British Museum/The Art Archive. 9 Olive Pearson. 10 British Museum/Michael Holford. 11 Chris Forsey, T; Robert Harding, B. 12 Abbas/Magnum. 13 British Museum, T; Musee du Louvre, Paris/The Art Archive, B. 14-15 AKG. 15 Ashmolean Museum, Oxford/ Werner Forman Archive. 16 British Museum/Michael Holford. 17 AKG/Erich Lessing. 18 British Museum/The Art Archive. 19 Staatliche Museum, Berlin/BPK, L; British Museum/ Werner Forman Archive, R. 20 Olive Pearson. 21 Ashmolean Museum/Werner Forman Archive. 22 Egyptian Museum, Cairo/The Art Archive. 23 Jurgen Liepe. 24-5 AKG. 26 Egyptian Museum, Cairo/The Art Archive. 27 Ashmolean Museum, Oxford/Bridgeman Art Library. 28 Trip/R.

Cracknell. 31 Egyptian Museum, Cairo/The Art Archive, T; Chris Forsey, B. 32 Bridgeman Art Library, B; Museum of Fine Arts, Boston/AKG, T. 33 Cheops Barque Museum/Werner Forman Archive. 34 Egyptian Museum, Cairo/BPK. 35 Egyptian Museum, Cairo/AKG. 36 Egyptian Museum, Cairo/ BPK. 37 Egyptian Museum, Cairo/Jurgen Liepe. 38 Luxor Museum/Jurgen Liepe. 39 Michael Holford. 40 Musee du Louvre, Paris/Bridgeman Art Library. 41 Egyptian Museum, Cairo/Jurgen Liepe. 42 Olive Pearson. 43 British Museum/ Werner Forman Archive. 44 Archaeological Museum, Khartoum/Werner Forman Archive. 45 Egyptian Museum, Cairo/Jurgen Liepe. 46 Robert Harding. 49 Sonia Halliday. 50 Robert Harding . 51 Olive Pearson. 52 Sonia Halliday. 53 British Museum/Michael Holford. 54 Egyptian National Museum/Giraudon/Bridgeman Art Library. 55 BPK. 56 British Museum/Michael Holford. 57 Egyptian Museum, Cairo/ Werner Forman Archive. 58 Egyptian Museum, Cairo/Jurgen Liepe. 59 Egyptian Museum, Cairo/Robert Harding. 60 Musee du Louvre, Paris/ Bridgeman Art

Library. 61 AKG. 62 Egyptian Museum, Cairo/ BPK. 63 British Museum/ Michael Holford. 64 Michael Holford. 65 AKG. 66-7 Paul Lowe/Magnum. 68 AKG. 69 Trip/D. Maybury. 70 Vorderasiatisches Museum/ BPK. 73 British Museum/The Art Archive. 74-75 British Museum/Michael Holford. 76-7 British Museum/AKG. 78-9 British Museum/AKG. 80 Akademie der Bildenden Kuenste, Vienna/AKG. 81 Egyptian Museum, Cairo/ Werner Forman Archive. 82 British Museum/AKG. 83 Olive Pearson. 84 Egyptian Museum, Cairo/BPK. 85 Egyptian Museum, Cairo/Jurgen Liepe. 86 Chris Forsey. 87 Staatliche Museum, Berlin/Werner Forman Archive. 88 Egyptian Museum, Cairo/Jurgen Liepe. 89 Staatliche Museum, Berlin/BPK. 90 Graeco-Roman Museum, Alexandria/Werner Forman Archive. 91Egyptian Museum, Cairo/BPK. 92 Michael Holford. 93 Kobal Collection, T; Musee du Louvre, Paris/Bridgeman Art Library, B.

	3000	2900	2800	2700	2600	2500	2400	2300	2200	2100	2000	1900	1800	1700	1600	1500	1400

Pre-dynastic: before 3150	Early Dynastic Period 3150–2686	OLD KINGDOM 2686–2181	First Intermediate Period: 2134–2023	MIDDLE KINGDOM 2033–1650	Second Intermediate Period: 1660–1570	NEW KINGDOM 1570–1070

• Unification of Egypt by **Narmer**

• **Djoser**

• **Pepy II**

• Great Pyramid at Giza built

• First pyramid built at Saqqara

• **Menthuhotep II**

• Nile floods bring famine

• the Hyksos

• **Amenemhat III**

• **Ahmose I**

• Bronze working introduced

• **Hatshepsut**

Contents

1 **THE FIRST KINGDOMS** 6

2 **THE AGE OF PYRAMIDS** 28

3 **THE RICHES OF EMPIRE** 46

4 **EGYPT AND THE NEW EMPIRES** 70

FURTHER INFORMATION 94

INDEX 94

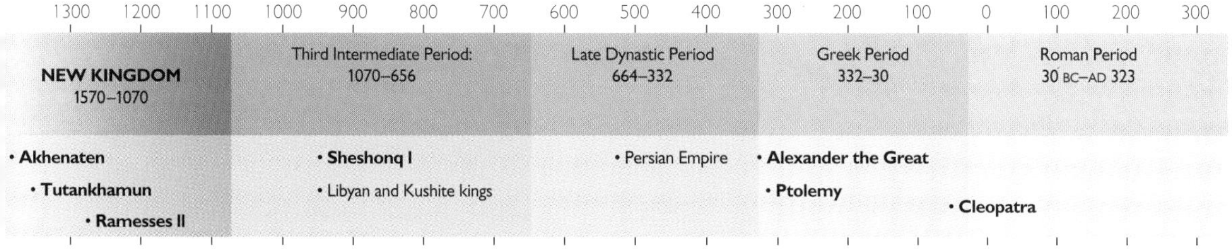

1300	1200	1100	1000	900	800	700	600	500	400	300	200	100	0	100	200	300

NEW KINGDOM 1570–1070			Third Intermediate Period: 1070–656				Late Dynastic Period 664–332			Greek Period 332–30			Roman Period 30 BC–AD 323			

- **Akhenaten**
  - **Tutankhamun**
    - **Ramesses II**
- **Sheshonq I**
  - Libyan and Kushite kings
- Persian Empire
- **Alexander the Great**
  - **Ptolemy**
    - **Cleopatra**

THE FIRST
KINGDOMS

1 THE FIRST KINGDOMS

Large agricultural settlements existed in Egypt and western Asia for thousands of years before 'urban' society and states developed. The two earliest major centres that archaeologists have examined are Jericho, where the first walled village was built about 9000 BC, and Chatal Huyuk in Turkey, dating from 7000–6000 BC. Elsewhere, throughout Mesopotamia, western Asia and the Nile Valley, were smaller agricultural communities with increasingly sophisticated cultures. Pottery was first made about 7000 BC. Then, around 3500 BC, towns and larger states appeared all over the region. This was followed by the invention of writing. Monumental buildings and more hierarchical societies are a feature of this new age. Rapidly the urban centres were brought together into full-scale cities under the rule of one individual with near god-like status. But what brought about this change to urban society and large states?

Previous page: Nebamun, an official of Egypt's imperial age, hunts in the marshes. Such scenes are often found in tomb chapels and symbolize the conquest of the forces of chaos by the deceased.

THE 'FERTILE CRESCENT'

The rich agricultural lands of two regions gave rise from around 3500 BC to the towns and early states of western Asia: the Nile Valley and the great sweep of territory often called the 'Fertile Crescent'. This arches from the head of the Persian Gulf, through Mesopotamia (modern Iraq) and northern Syria, to the Mediterranean coast, continuing south through modern Lebanon and Israel. The Fertile Crescent was flanked by regions rich in natural resources. The mountains of Anatolia (the Asian part of modern Turkey), Lebanon and northern Syria had thick forests of pine and cedar. Farther north, along the coast of the Black Sea, were forests of deciduous trees. The differing environments and available resources of the Fertile Crescent helped to shape the types of settlement and agriculture that people adopted and developed there.

Mesopotamia, lying between the rivers Tigris and Euphrates, became home to the two great kingdoms of Babylonia and Assyria. Although Babylon came to dominate the south, there were many other ancient towns there. Originally, the coast of the Persian Gulf was probably much farther north than it is at present, and the river

FERTILE CRESCENT

1

courses of the Tigris and Euphrates were different, meeting farther north and then following several channels to the sea. This would have left Ur and Eridu as the southernmost cities.

Forests and desert

Mesopotamia had little good timber, so early building relied on reeds and mud brick. Although rich agriculturally, the country lacked many other important resources. There was little stone available and there were no sources of metals, so these had to be imported from surrounding or distant regions. By contrast, timber and metals were found in abundance in the lands to the north and west of Mesopotamia: a swathe of territory including the mountainous regions of Armenia,

northern Syria and Anatolia, stretching west as far as the Levantine shore of the Mediterranean and south as far as modern Lebanon. The mountains of Lebanon, which come down almost to the sea, were a major source of good-quality timber. There were also pine forests in Syria and extensive forests of ash, birch and oak in Anatolia and in the region between the Black Sea and Caspian Sea.

The northernmost regions were also the principal sources of copper and iron, and here a series of great powers developed, such as the Hittite empire in Anatolia and the kingdom of Mitanni in northern Syria. Farther south, the hillier lands of Palestine were also wooded. Changes in climate and intensive human activity have since altered much of the land. Animal life, too, has changed due to the increased desert and the impact of humans.

Previous page:
The Fertile Crescent stretched from the Persian Gulf to the Mediterranean coast, and included the river courses of the Tigris and Euphrates.

1. The 'Standard' of Ur has inlaid scenes of war and peace made of shell and lapis lazuli.

2. The ziggurats of southern Mesopotamia were solid and crowned by a temple.

2

▷ THE ZIGGURAT AT UR

As soon as societies were organized in towns, humans began to build large structures. Mud brick was the most common building material in Egypt and Mesopotamia. The structures that survive were generally built as temples or tombs. The great ziggurat of Ur (pictured right) was built by Ur-Nammu around 2100 BC as a temple to the moon god Nanna. It measures 64 by 46 m (210 by 151 ft) at the base, and was originally three storeys high with a small temple structure on top. Built of sun-dried mud brick and faced with burnt brick, the ziggurat is a solid mountain with no internal chambers. As we see it now, it was enlarged by King Nabonidus of Babylon (555–539 BC). The ziggurat has been restored recently.

The elephant was once widespread in western Asia. As late as 1450 BC, the Egyptian pharaoh Thutmose III hunted elephants in the valley of the Orontes, which runs north through Syria to the Mediterranean. Elephants had become extinct there by 1000 BC.

The Fertile Crescent is fringed on its southern edge by desert stretching south into Arabia and Sinai. Arabia came into prominence later, when the incense trade from the far south became important. The mountainous region of Sinai was a source of two precious materials – turquoise and copper – and became a focus of Egyptian activity from early times. Sinai also protected Egypt from invasion from Asia.

THE GIFT OF THE NILE

Egypt owes its existence to the Nile. Before the building of the Aswan Dam (1960–1970), the river flooded for three months of every year, from late July to September; the flood waters then receded from October onwards. This inundation covered the whole of the Nile Valley with a layer of rich mud and saturated the ground, making it ideal for the cultivation of crops. But the flood was unpredictable, relying as it did on the rains at the river's sources farther south, so there was always the possiblity of drought and subsequent famine.

1. Although the Nile Valley is quite narrow, it is a very rich agricultural land.

2. From an 18th-Dynasty papyrus roll. The fat blue figure of Hapy represents the fertility of the Nile flood.

3. The hippopotamus was a danger to humans and damager of crops. This glazed earthenware model dates from c.2000–1900 BC.

1

The White Nile rises in Lake Victoria and flows northwards through Uganda into the vast swampland of southern Sudan, known as the Sudd; the Blue Nile has its source in Lake Tana, in the highlands of Ethiopia. The two rivers meet at Khartoum in Sudan and their united stream is soon joined by the River Atbara, which also comes from the Ethiopian highlands. The Nile then loops its way through Nubia, a vast and desolate sandstone plateau, much of it desert, stretching east as far as the Red Sea, and fringed to the west by the Libyan Desert and to the north by southern Egypt. It is the two rivers from Ethiopia that bring the silt. For the ancient Egyptians, if the rains failed in the

Ethiopian highlands, the Nile floods were low, bringing famine and other problems. Equally, if the waters were too high, there could be devastation throughout the country. Control of the Nile flood has always been essential to Egypt's productivity.

The cataracts

As the Nile flows northwards, twisting in great bends through the savanna of Sudan and the Nubian Desert, natural features carve its length into units. The Nubian stretch of the valley is divided into different regions by the cataracts, where underlying hard granite breaks through the soft sandstone on the surface, forming islands and rapids in the river that can make navigation impossible. The cataracts are numbered from north to south (contrary to the flow of the river), the first being at Aswan. From the First Cataract north as far as the Mediterranean, there are no further major obstacles to navigation, except sandbanks.

Following the river north towards the sea, the next main natural division after the First Cataract is in the region of Gebel Silsila, where sandstone cliffs come down on both sides of the Nile. A little way north of Silsila the stone changes to limestone, which is harder and creates a different landscape. The Nile has cut a deep, broad valley through the limestone hills, with high cliffs, usually on the east bank, and broad alluvial deposits on the west. A natural offshoot leaves the Nile near Asyut and runs parallel with it before turning into the Fayum – a huge natural depression in Egypt's Western Desert, sinking at its lowest point to 45 m (150 ft)

1. The staple grain crops of Egypt were wheat for bread and barley for beer. Women gleaning the fallen ears of corn follow the reapers in a painting from the 18th Dynasty.

below sea level – where it creates a lake. Farther north again, the Nile passes beyond the limestone plateau. This is where, before the building of the Aswan Dam, it started to deposit its silt, forming the Nile Delta. For much of Egyptian history, the Nile Delta was fringed with thick swamp, not unlike the marshes of southern Iraq, and the seven major branches of the river divided the swamp into large islands.

The Delta formed the kingdom of Lower Egypt; the Nile Valley from Memphis, just south of the apex of the Delta, and continuing south as far as the First Cataract comprised the kingdom of Upper Egypt. The whole region of North Africa has

 CONTROLLING THE NILE

The organization of labour and the storing of surplus food were among the prime concerns of Egypt's rulers. It was the role of the pharaoh – the title given to the kings of a unified Egypt – to control (as a god) the Nile flood, ensuring that it was neither too high nor too low; the pharaoh was also (as king) responsible for the construction of dykes and canals, as well as for their maintenance. If the canals were not properly cleared, the fields would become affected by salination, or the dykes might break, causing the water to flood the land and destroying crops. The ceremonial mace head attributed to King 'Scorpion' (pictured below) shows the king performing a ceremony relating to the 'inundation', as the flood was known.

suffered from increasingly arid conditions since the end of the last Ice Age, and these have affected the Nile Valley and its surrounding regions. We can be fairly certain that when communities were developing here in the period from 5000 to 3000 BC, the areas that are now deserts, particularly those to the west of the Nile, were savanna or scrubland that supported a rich variety of wildlife. Rock drawings and paintings on pottery from that period show elephants, giraffe, ostriches and types of antelope that we now think of as belonging much farther south. Throughout Egyptian history, crocodiles and hippopotamuses were a danger to the people of the valley.

Egypt's natural resources

As well as enabling agriculture, the annual deposits of mud also provided Egypt with its main building material. Low rainfall allowed the Egyptians to use mud bricks that were simply dried in the sun. Houses built of sun-dried mud brick could be rebuilt easily and cheaply, and were warm in winter and cool in summer. Throughout Egyptian history, mud brick was used for all types of building, from royal palaces and frontier fortresses to the simplest houses of agricultural labourers.

Flanked by limestone cliffs and sandstone hills, Egypt (unlike Mesopotamia) had easy access to stone, and large-scale stone architecture developed there before anywhere else in the Near East. Despite being easily available, stone was used primarily for structures that were intended to endure – the temples of the gods and the tombs of the dead. In houses, stone was used for the most important features, such as the doorways and the bases of the columns in the main rooms.

Although there were ample supplies of mud and stone, Egypt had relatively little good timber. The native trees, principally the date palm and tamarisk, could be used for roofs and for strengthening walls, but were not good enough to make fine furniture, statues or ships. So Egypt, even in very early times, imported most of the timber it needed from Asia.

The deserts surrounding Egypt were rich in natural materials. As well as sandstone and lime-stone, there was granite, both in the desert and at the First Cataract. There were also more decorative stones, such as alabaster and quartzite. Large blocks of stone could be moved easily over long distances during the flood season using large rafts or shallow-bottom boats, and the use of massive pieces of stone quickly became a characteristic of Egyptian architecture. Semi-precious coloured stones such as red carnelian could also be found in Egypt's Eastern Desert between the Nile and the Red Sea, and the Egyptians sent expeditions to Sinai to bring back turquoise from the mines. Most importantly, gold was abundant in the Eastern Desert and in Nubia to the south. Gold was to play an essential role in Egypt's relations with other

1. A wall painting from around 1300 BC shows sculptors at work in the temple workshops. They are fashioning a vessel and a sphinx.

2. (opposite) Metal-workers smelt bronze to cast a door and brickmakers exploit Egypt's most abundant natural material – mud.

countries. There were not, however, abundant supplies of other metals such as copper or iron. These, too, were imported from much farther afield. Other commodities were highly valued for their decorative nature. Ebony and ivory, for example, were used to make furniture. Both were brought along the Nile route from the southern part of Nubia and from East Africa. Incense (important at a time when there was no soap) was gathered from a variety of plants, some of which grew only in Ethiopia.

FROM VILLAGES TO STATES

From about 5000 BC, agricultural communities were scattered the length of the Nile Valley from the Delta south as far as Nubia. River travel eased communication between the settlements, and the culture of these separate regions became increasingly unified. Fine pottery, stone vessels and jewellery were being produced, some of which show characteristics that would become familiar in later Egyptian art. It is also clear that there were

 IVORY

Ivory was always highly prized as a material for furniture and for other prestige objects. The picture on the left shows an ivory panel with Egyptian-inspired decoration from an 8th-century BC Phoenician throne. The tusks of hippopotamuses were a common source of ivory, but the tusks of elephants were much larger and therefore more easily worked. In the earliest periods, elephants were still found in Nubia, but as they were forced farther and farther south by arid conditions, and also probably by hunting, ivory had to be brought from further afield. The Egyptian name for the island and town at the First Cataract of the Nile, marking their country's southern border, was Abu, which means 'elephant' or 'ivory'. This town began as a major centre for trade between the kingdom of Nekhen (Hierakonpolis) and Nubia.

strong contacts between the Nile Delta and western Asia, and between southern Egypt and Nubia. The welding of villages and regions into the earliest states began some time after 4000 BC.

Current excavation in Egypt is finding more and more fascinating material from this early period when the first kingdoms emerged. The evidence is pushing back the date of these early societies and also showing their remarkable complexity and sophistication. Our knowledge of the Nile Delta region is still much more limited than that of Upper (southern) Egypt. This is partly due to the survival – or non-survival – of archaeological material and the environmental conditions. The Delta sites are usually in areas of cultivation and in much wetter situations, making excavation and preservation more difficult; in Upper Egypt, by contrast, the cemeteries and some of the town sites are on the edge of the desert where the dry sand preserves a huge range of different types of artefacts and organic material. The development of states may, in part, have been stimulated by climatic change.

1. A pottery vessel decorated with boats from c.3500–3000 BC during the Predynastic period.

2. Part of the 'Battlefield Palette' showing slain figures scavenged by vultures and a lion. It comes from the centuries immediately preceding the unification of Egypt in 3100 BC.

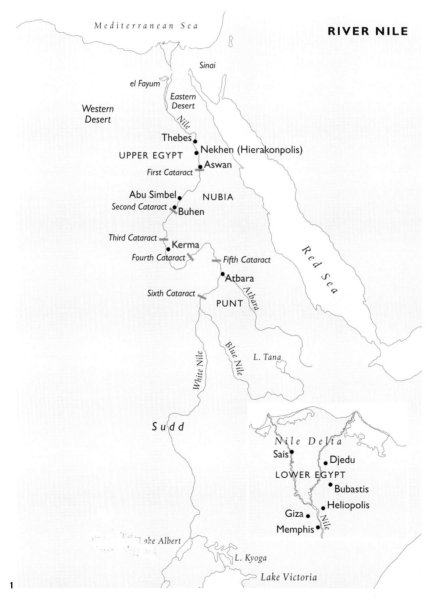

RIVER NILE

1. The White Nile, rising in Lake Victoria, is joined by the Blue Nile and the Atbara from the Ethiopian highlands, and the united stream flows towards the Mediterranean Sea. In the Nubian stretch of the Nile Valley, the river is divided into different regions by the cataracts (stretches with numerous rapids).

2. This large pottery lion from Hierakonpolis combines stylization with naturalism. It probably dates from the Early Dynastic period, or 3rd Dynasty.

2

Artisans and élites

There is some indication that from around 3300 BC conditions became drier, which forced scattered settlements into more densely populated areas. So, for example, at Hierakonpolis in Upper Egypt, archaeological evidence suggests that a more scattered settlement, which originally extended across the flood plain and into the wadi (a valley running from the plain into the desert hills), was replaced by a town. In Upper Egypt three main centres emerged in the later Predynastic period (up to about 3100 BC): at Abydos, Naqada and Hierakonpolis. There were, presumably, other similar 'chiefdoms' scattered throughout the Nile Valley and Delta. The consensus among Egyptologists used to be that the process of unification was violent and the result of a series of prolonged wars between north and south. Many archaeologists now think differently: the evidence shows that the country had already become culturally unified by the time it was politically united under one king.

The greater density of population would have allowed further exploitation of the agricultural potential of the Nile's flooding, and could also have led to a more structured and hierarchical society. The increased agricultural surplus provided for those who were not engaged in agriculture, such as the artisans and the new élites that consisted of priests and controllers of trade. The concentration of specialist artisans and other groups who were in a controlling position saw the development of a new range of artistic and architectural forms. These included the elaborate tombs for members of the élites and objects made from materials such as ebony and ivory, which were the result of long-distance exchange.

The painted pottery and other objects from this period of the first kingdoms show that a distinctive Egyptian artistic style was beginning to form. Egyptian religion was also developing some of its later characteristics. There is evidence of early temple structures at Hierakonpolis, and the painted pottery shows boats with recognizable emblems of the gods. One of the commonest of these is the thunderbolt of the fertility god Min, who is also represented in some of the earliest statues of gods.

Palettes and mace heads

The earliest Egyptian monuments that show kings in the style characteristic of their successors are ceremonial palettes and mace heads (such as the 'Scorpion' mace head, ▷ p. 15), which were offered in the temple of Hierakonpolis. Ordinary palettes were flat, shield-shaped pieces of stone, usually a type of schist (siltstone), which were used to grind eye-paint. The ceremonial palettes were much bigger and had carved decoration on both sides. The palette of Narmer shows the king – one of the earliest pharaohs of a united Egypt – wearing the white crown, the emblem of kingship over Upper

 MUMMIFICATION

The dry, sandy desert of Egypt naturally preserved the bodies of the dead. Excavated graves of the later Predynastic period contain bodies surrounded by pottery and foodstuffs. When larger tombs with burial chambers began to be used, a new method of preservation had to be developed. The earliest known mummies are from the Old Kingdom (2686–2181 BC), but the process was not perfected until the New Kingdom (1570–1070 BC), with the discovery of natron, a compound of sodium carbonate, sodium bicarbonate and sodium chloride (salt). Mummification became increasingly elaborate, the internal organs being removed and preserved separately. Many protective amulets (charms) were included in the wrappings, and the face was covered with a mask, like the one on the right, belonging to an 18th-Dynasty princess. There were one or more painted coffins and these, too, became increasingly elaborate, covered with scenes showing the deceased in front of Osiris, judge of the dead. The body was preserved as a home for the soul, but preserving the name of the dead was also essential. This conferred immortality, but also enabled the soul to find its proper abode.

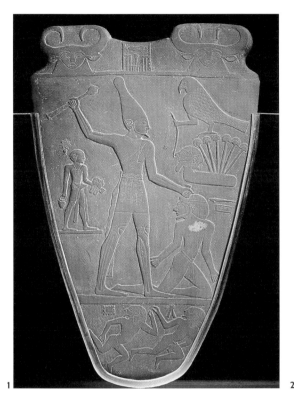

1

2

1. In the scenes on the ceremonial palette of King Narmer, the conventions of Egyptian art appear alongside the imagery of the Egyptian kingship. Here Narmer, wearing the white crown of Upper Egypt, smites an enemy.

2. Narmer, wearing the red crown of Lower Egypt, is preceded by the standards of the gods. Beneath, in the form of a bull, he overthrows a town.

Egypt. He is smiting a kneeling captive, with his sandal-bearer standing behind him and the falcon god Horus in front.

The other side is divided into three distinct registers (a feature typical of later Egyptian art), one of which shows the king as a bull battering a walled enclosure. Narmer also appears wearing the red crown, the symbol of Lower Egypt, preceded by the standards of gods borne on poles and by an official who carries the title 'vizier'. Again, he is followed by his sandal-bearer, who was always close by to take the king's sandals during the performance of religious rites. The central register of the whole side has two animals with long, intertwined necks, of Mesopotamian inspiration.

The city of Memphis

Our knowledge of Lower (northern) Egypt is still inadequate, but excavations at Buto in the western Nile Delta show strong cultural links with western Asia. The unification of Egypt is generally believed to have taken several generations. For the Egyptians themselves, it was marked according to later tradition by the founding of the city of Memphis. The unification of the country and the founding of Memphis were both attributed to a king known as Meni (in Greek, Menes). Meni may be a composite king, representing all those, such as Scorpion and Narmer, who brought the whole country under their rule. Memphis is the Greek name, derived from the Egyptian name Men-nofer, but the town was originally called Inbu-hedj, the 'White Castle'. It was built at the controlling point of Egypt, just south of where the Nile Valley and the Delta join, and in consequence it was called 'The Balance of the Two Lands'. Memphis itself remained the chief city of Egypt until Alexander the Great founded Alexandria in 332 BC.

The influence of geography

The civilizations of ancient Egypt and Mesopotamia were both the result of large rivers that provided rich flood plains with annual inundations. In both regions, to use the rivers to their full advantage, intensive canal construction was necessary to drain the land and to provide water for irrigation. There were differences, however. In Mesopotamia, the flood came in the spring, coinciding with the ripening and harvesting of crops. There was the danger of losing crops through flooding, and so canals were needed to take off excess water. In Egypt the flood came in the height of summer. The land was ploughed and crops were sown soon after; in good years this gave farmers time to gather in the harvest before the next flood.

1

1. Winnowing grain before it is taken to the state storehouses. The labourers use fans (scoops that fit the hand) to throw the grain into the air, allowing the wind to carry away the chaff (or husks).

2. Crushing grapes and collecting the juice to make wine. Wine was made in Egypt from about 2900 BC onwards. The Nile Delta was the prime wine-producing region.

Another important factor was the speed at which the rivers flowed. The Tigris is swifter than the Euphrates, so most settlements in southern Mesopotamia were built closer to the Euphrates, either along its banks, or on canals running from it. The course of the two rivers allowed towns to develop throughout the broad flood plain. In Egypt, by contrast, the single broad expanse of the Nile, for much of its length close to cliffs rising on its eastern flank, dictated a more linear settlement pattern.

Elsewhere in the Near East, the coastal cities of Phoenicia (southern Lebanon and northern Israel) were either on the narrow strip of land between the mountains and the sea, or on islands close to the shore. These cities had little accessible agricultural land and developed as trading cities. Throughout the mountains, hills and steppe lands of Syria, Palestine and Anatolia, settlement was scattered. In Mesopotamia and western Asia, the majority of agricultural labourers lived in the towns and walked to their fields. In western Asia, Egypt and Nubia, there were cattle herders as well as arable farmers. In many regions of western Asia, these people were semi-nomadic, moving with their herds on the margins of the cultivated land. In Egypt and Nubia the herders were an essential part of the economy and some regions, such as the Nile Delta, were used for grazing cattle.

Wealth and bureaucracy

Despite their differing patterns of settlement, the societies that developed in western Asia had similarities. They were all ruled by élites who controlled religious and political life and accumulated wealth through taxation and tribute. This

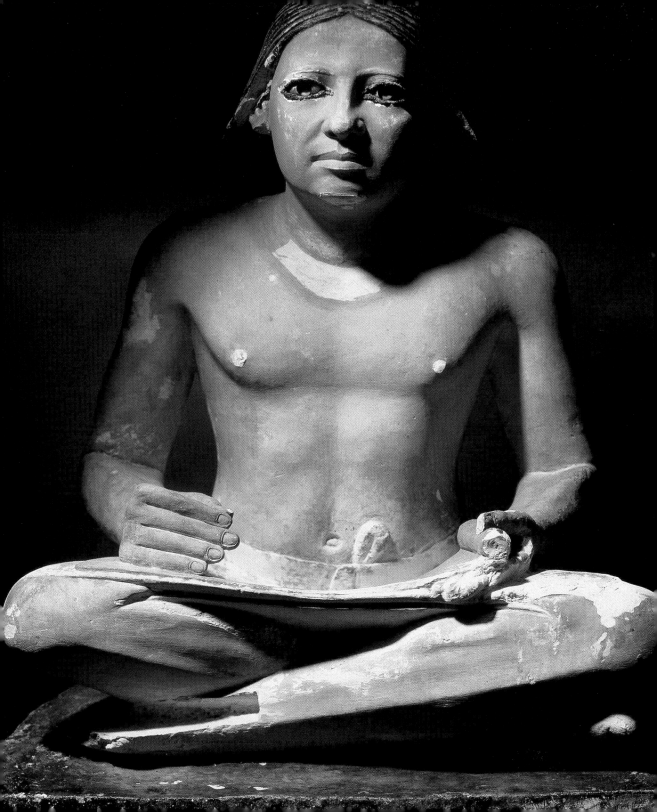

2

wealth was soon being spent on the construction of monumental public buildings, which gave legitimacy to the society and to its rulers. The surplus production from intensive agriculture supported craftworkers and skilled specialists. The desire for materials stimulated long-distance trade and the development of complex exchange economies that soon made the new cities dependent on each other.

Under such conditions, there was a need to keep track of agricultural production, taxation and trade. In both Mesopotamia and Egypt, systems of writing were developed. The early scribes started with pictograms – 'pictures' of what they wanted to record. Where commercial exchange was taking place across a multilingual region, these had the advantage of not being embedded in a single tongue. Over time, simpler scripts were developed. The Mesopotamian 'cuneiform' used a script of wedge-shaped marks made by a wooden stylus (stick) in soft, wet clay, which was then baked hard. In Egypt, an early form of the hieroglyphic script, also based on pictorial signs, is found on slate palettes and on ivory and bone labels from tombs, documenting the goods buried. These signs (commonly known by the Greek word *hieroglyph*, 'sacred sign') some-times represent the object they resemble, but also came to stand for particular sounds or groups of sounds. Soon, the papyrus plant was being used to manufacture a type of paper, and new scripts were developed for writing in ink prepared from watered soot, allowing Egypt to create one of the great bureaucracies of the ancient world.

1. (opposite) The classic image of the Egyptian scribe, sitting cross-legged, his papyrus roll spread on his lap and his pen poised to write. In Egypt, writing was power.

2. In Mesopotamia clay tablets were used for correspondence and administrative documents. This tablet carries a record in early Sumerian of quantities of produce.

THE AGE OF PYRAMIDS

THE AGE OF PYRAMIDS

Thirty dynasties ruled Egypt between its first unification in 3100 BC and its conquest by Alexander the Great in 332 BC. During the three phases when the country was united – known as the Old, Middle and New Kingdoms – there was only one king and ruling dynasty at a time. Between these phases there were times of disunity, known as Intermediate Periods, when rival dynasties ruled in different parts of Egypt. The Egyptians manipulated their past by listing their rulers as if they had reigned in one unbroken line from the time of the gods. For political and religious reasons, some rulers were omitted from the lists – the most notable omissions were the female pharaoh Hatshepsut, and the 'heretic' Akhenaten. It was during the Old and Middle Kingdoms that the most impressive of the royal pyramid tombs were built, bearing witness to this day to the awesome achievements of the Egypt of the pharaohs.

Previous page: The vast scale of the Sphinx and Pyramid of Khafre at Giza epitomizes the remote, god-like status of the pharaohs of the Old Kingdom.

A UNIFIED EGYPT

In reality, the unification of Egypt was almost certainly a piecemeal process that took place over several centuries. Later generations of Egyptians, however, saw it differently. For them, perhaps because of the country's tendency to divide into two in periods of crisis, the coming together of Upper Egypt (the south) and Lower Egypt (the north) was the most important event in their history – which they attributed to the possibly mythical figure of Pharaoh Meni (▷ p. 24).

The imagery of Upper and Lower Egypt and its binding together became a constant theme of Egyptian art and religion, a response to that underlying tension. It was portrayed as a blending and balancing out of the different traditions associated with the north and south. Symbolizing it was the double crown of the pharaohs, combining the tall red crown of Lower Egypt with the conical white crown of Upper Egypt.

1

1. The falcon-god Horus extends his protective wings around his earthly manifestation, the 4th-Dynasty pharaoh Khafre.

2. The names of three 4th-Dynasty pharaohs enclosed in an oval ring (known as a 'cartouche'), which symbolized eternity.

God-kings

The characteristics we associate with ancient Egypt began to appear quickly after unification. The pharaoh was supreme ruler and living representative of the gods on Earth, and had a role both as an administrator and as a priest. On a practical level, he was responsible for the control of the Nile and the food supply; on the spiritual level, his divine power and relationship with the gods ensured a good flood each year. The king, usually referred to as pharaoh (from the Egyptian term meaning 'great

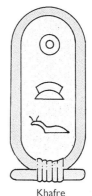
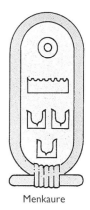

2   Khufu   Khafre   Menkaure

house' or 'palace'), ruled a small population of about 1.5 million people in the early period – up to about 2000 BC. He was attended by a small group of élite families, many related to him; these may have numbered little more than 2000 people altogether.

The pharaoh spent much of his time travelling the country to celebrate festivals of the gods. The regulation of his life is reflected in the increasing formality of the buildings associated with him, which often have a symmetrical plan and are oriented on a strict north-south axis. For his public appearances he was attended by fan-bearers, indicating his divine status. Among his officials, there was no division into professions. They had to perform priestly service for a set number of days each month. The same officials might lead military or quarrying expeditions, or they might oversee matters of law, tax and administration.

1

 THE STEP PYRAMID

The Step Pyramid of Djoser (left), constructed in 2660 BC, was designed by the architect Imhotep. In its earliest form, the pyramid was a large, flat-topped tomb (*mastaba*) like that of the earlier kings. It was later enlarged with two more layers, then increased even further. It was built of relatively small blocks of stone and encased in a fine-grained, brilliant white limestone. The pyramid was surrounded by a complex of buildings, which were little more than façades on a solid mass of masonry. This is because the structures were built for eternity, to be inhabited by the spirit world rather than for use by the living.

2

Old Kingdom pyramids

The pharaoh controlled resources such as stone, and soon the royal burial places and their temples became the main focus of labour and expenditure. The early kings had tombs of mud brick at Abydos in southern Egypt, but after the 3rd Dynasty came to power in 2686 BC the royal cemetery was moved north to the desert plateau overlooking the city of Memphis. Here, the Step Pyramid of Djoser marked a significant new departure: it was the first venture into large-scale stone architecture. The new architecture developed rapidly, producing the 'true' pyramids of Medum, Dashur and Giza in the 4th Dynasty (c.2613–2494 BC). At Giza the Great Pyramid and its successors were surrounded by streets of tombs for officials; the size of a tomb depended on the rank of the official and his personal relationship with the king.

Most of the building work was carried out during the Nile's annual flooding. The bulk of the stone was quarried at the desert plateau site above the Nile's west bank, but a finer white limestone used for the casing came from a quarry on the east bank. The high flood waters enabled the stone to be floated on rafts and shallow-bottom boats across the river to the edge of the desert, where a causeway led up to the plateau. While men worked on the constructions, their families were fed from the state supplies.

Pyramid-building continued in much the same way in the 5th and 6th Dynasties (2494–2181 BC). By this time, however, the power of the pharaoh was declining. Power appears to have shifted from

1. Although shown in the conventional pose of husband and wife, King Menkaure and Queen Kamerernebty have a remote, austere air.

2. The cedar-wood boat of Khufu, found dismantled in a pit adjacent to the Great Pyramid, typifies the elegance of the Old Kingdom.

the centre to the regions, and local nobles seem to have increased their authority. This is indicated by the absence of officials' tombs surrounding royal pyramids of this period, and the existence of large tombs in remote provincial towns.

The rise of Thebes

The crisis that brought the Old Kingdom to an end is thought to have come in the reign of Pepy II, which lasted about 96 years, the longest recorded reign of any ancient Egyptian king. By the time of his death in 2184 BC, the power of the local nobility had grown hugely and was still rising. The situation was perhaps aggravated by low Nile levels and increased drying of the Sahara.

A new dynasty, the 7th, succeeded Pepy, ruling from Herakleopolis, to the south of Memphis. Its kings were acknowledged as legitimate pharaohs, but they seem to have had little influence outside the north. There is evidence of conflict between the armies of local rulers, some of whom employed Nubian mercenary soldiers. Later records portray this period – the First Intermediate Period – as one in which the accepted order was turned upside down. The main opposition to the pharaohs of Herakleopolis came from the southern princedom of Thebes. Thebes, however, was flanked by powerful governors who were loyal to the pharaoh, at Nekhen to its south and around Abydos to its north, and it took the Theban rulers some time to expand their princedom. But eventually they assumed royal titles and open war with the kings of the north became inevitable.

1

1. Convention dictated that men were depicted as redbrown and women as a creamy yellow.

2. In this funerary statue, King Menthuhotep II is painted black, the colour of rebirth.

THE MIDDLE KINGDOM

From about 2000 BC, the self-styled kings of Thebes extended their control southwards to Aswan and northwards into central Egypt, in a series of campaigns led by Inyotef II, who reigned for nearly 50 years. His grandson Menthuhotep II, in a reign of equal length, was able to reunite Egypt, marking the beginning of the Middle Kingdom.

The triumph of the Theban rulers marks the beginning of their home town's importance. In 1985 BC, a new dynasty, the 12th, came to power. This family maintained strong associations with Thebes, and its kings built extensively there. But they also established a royal residence and administrative city in the north at Itjet-tawy, a little to the south of Memphis, as well as building their pyramid tombs in the north.

Centralizing the state

The Middle Kingdom pharaohs reorganized the administration of Egypt. The old system of principalities (usually known by the Greek term *nomes*) was replaced by a more centralized administration with two divisions, each headed by a vizier. The vizier of Lower Egypt controlled the region extending from the Nile Delta as far south as Akhmim; the vizier of Upper Egypt controlled the country from Akhmim south into Nubia. Many old families appear to have retained their local importance, however. One significant change was that the king's brothers and sons no longer held the most important offices of state.

When complete, the Great Pyramid at Giza contained about 2,300,000 blocks of stone, each averaging 2.5 tonnes in weight. The maximum weight of a block was 15 tonnes.

2

1

LAPIS LAZULI

Lapis lazuli is a dark blue stone that was much used in Egyptian jewellery of all periods. The nearest source of lapis was in Afghanistan, and it was therefore the product of very long-distance trade. Blue was a protective colour and was also associated with sky gods. The dark blue of lapis and the brighter colour of turquoise were imitated in opaque glass paste. The bracelet of Tutankhamun (pictured below) has a large scarab beetle of lapis lazuli. The scarab was a popular motif as it represented one of the forms of the sun god. The scarab (the Egyptian word is *kheper*) also formed part of Tutankhamun's throne-name, Neb-kheperu-re.

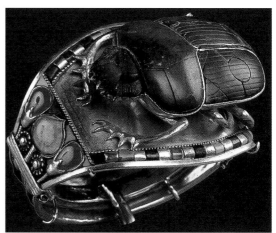

Middle Kingdom architecture

Once again the royal funerary complex, focusing on a pyramid, became the centre of state labour. The Middle Kingdom pyramids were large, but built of rubble or brick encased in finer quality stone. The temple complexes attached to them were very large and elaborate. The most spectacular was that of Amenemhat III at Hawara, which reputedly contained individual temples for each of the district gods of Egypt, and used a variety of different types of stone from all over the country. Quarrying expeditions sent by Middle Kingdom pharaohs are recorded in rock inscriptions scattered around Egypt and its surrounding regions, from the amethyst mines of the Wadi el-Hudi in Nubia to the turquoise and copper mines of Sinai.

Middle Kingdom architecture, particularly in the 12th Dynasty (1985–1795 BC), was elegant and refined. Sculpture was striking, frequently carved in very hard stones. The faces of the pharaohs lack the calm, other-worldly gaze of the Old Kingdom figures; instead, they reveal careworn rulers under the pressures of their office. Increased royal control and extensive building works stimulated artistic production. It was an age of prosperity, in part due to centralization and efficient control of the Nile flood, but also to Egypt's expansion south into Nubia, with its rich resources of raw materials.

TRADE AND CONQUEST

With one foot in the Mediterranean, Egypt had always looked outward to the civilizations of the Near East and beyond. Nubia, though, was all-African in its orientation. Its sun-scorched, rocky plateau was not then as barren as climate change has since made it. Even so, it could never have supported the rich agrarian economy of its neighbour Egypt. Instead, herdsmen grazed their cattle over limitless pastures. What cultivation there was hugged the banks of the Nile as it snaked across savanna and desert; there was no great fertile floodplain here of the sort to be found downriver.

1. The statues of the Middle Kingdom pharaohs, such as Amenemhat III, combine an idealized youthful body with the face of the care-worn mature ruler.

2. This pectoral carries the name of Amenemhat III and figures of the pharaoh smiting foreign enemies. The vulture goddess, Nekhbet, hovers protectively over the whole scene.

From the beginning, Egypt and Nubia developed side by side. The Nubians exchanged commodities such as ivory and perhaps some gold for Egyptian foodstuffs they could not produce in their own harsh climate. But once Egypt had united, its rulers initiated a more warlike policy, taking their armies into Nubia to gain direct control of its resources and trade. During the Old Kingdom, the Egyptians had a presence in Nubia at Buhen, at the foot of the Second Cataract. They seem to have conducted trade with the regions farther south in Africa from Buhen, while in the desert to Buhen's west lay the diorite quarries exploited in Egypt's 4th Dynasty.

Much later, during the Middle Kingdom, around the end of the 11th and the beginning of the 12th Dynasties (1985 BC), there is evidence that a powerful state developed in northern Nubia. At first, this kingdom seems to have maintained good relations with Egypt, but later hostilities broke out. The Egyptians eventually crushed the northern Nubian kingdom and moved to protect the Second Cataract, where they had lost their earlier foothold at Buhen. Their main interest seems to have been trade with the south. Under the 12th-Dynasty kings Senusret I and Senusret III, the Egyptians built a number of fortresses to protect the transit of trade through the Second Cataract, including a supply depot at Buhen.

At this time, southern Nubia was controlled by the kingdom of Kush, which lay in a fertile region south of the Third Cataract, with its main city at Kerma. It was in a good position to control the long-distance trade in ivory, ebony, incense and animal skins coming from the savanna of central Sudan and the mountains of Ethiopia. But any trade

passing north along the Nile was vulnerable to attack by the people living in Nubia's Eastern Desert. The Egyptians appear to have supported Kush as a major trading partner and this may have included military protection for convoys of goods. The Egyptians may also have begun to exploit the gold-producing regions of the Eastern Desert, and were certainly active in the amethyst mines at Wadi el-Hudi, southeast of Aswan.

The land of Punt

The Nile traffic was not the only African source of wealth that the 12th-Dynasty pharaohs fostered. An expedition along the coast of the Red Sea to the land of Punt is recorded in the reign of Amenemhat II (c.1922–1878 BC). Punt was a major source of incense, although gold and other luxuries also came from there. At one time Egyptologists placed

1. Senusret III assured Egypt's control of Nubia, and was later worshipped there as a god.

2. (opposite) The wealth of eastern Africa which came through Nubia: rings of gold, lumps of incense, logs of ebony, animal tails, cheetah skins and a baboon.

1

Punt in Somalia and the Horn of Africa, but it is now identified with a succession of political chiefdoms in the mountains of Ethiopia and eastern Sudan.

The most detailed account of a journey to Punt is that of the 18th-Dynasty female pharaoh, Hatshepsut (1472–1458 BC). Spectacular reliefs in her mortuary temple tell the full story of what she clearly regarded as not merely a trading venture but a triumphant vindication of her ability to do a male monarch's work. The strange animals and plants of this exotic land, its beehive houses, its black-skinned people and its proudly obese queen: everything that makes Punt more foreign is insisted upon in these elaborate scenes. So, too, is the produce with which

Hatshepsut journeyed home to enrich the Egyptian state. Incense, frankincense, myrrh and other perfumes, gold by the sackful, elephant tusks and ivory, leopard skins and even a band of monkeys: all are shown, being loaded onto the pharaoh's ships. As the inscription says, 'Never were brought such things to any king, since the world was.'

Asian contacts

Egypt's contacts with its neighbours in Africa are well documented. Less well known, but just as important, were its contacts with Asia. During the 12th Dynasty, Amenemhat I (1985–1955 BC)

 WORSHIPPING THE GODS

There were many temples in towns and villages, as well as wayside shrines and small chapels in remote places. All of these could be visited, although access to the inner parts was restricted to initiated priests. The temples were places of formal state worship, and the great gods were generally thought to be concerned with the harmony of the universe rather than the petty concerns of individuals. Therefore, much of Egyptian worship by the ordinary people took place in the home. There was a host of deities who protected the house from snakes, scorpions and illnesses, and some who specifically helped women during pregnancy and the dangerous time of childbirth. The most important of these gods were Bes (right), who took the form of a bandy-legged dwarf draped in a lion skin, poking out his tongue, and the fiercesome goddess Taweret, a pregnant hippopotamus with lion's paws and a crocodile's tail.

1. One of the most striking images from the record of Hatshepsut's expedition to Punt is that of the ruler's wife. Her size indicates her wealth, and also a very un-Egyptian sense of beauty.

1

defended the eastern border with a line of fortifi-
cations called the Walls of the Ruler. There are
indications that the Egyptian army was active at
this time in southern Palestine, but there is no real
evidence of imperial ambitions. Trade with old
partners, such as the port city of Byblos, north of
modern Beirut, was important for Egypt for the
acquisition of timber. In a temple at Tod, south of
Thebes, French archaeologists discovered a hoard of
145 silver vessels, with many silver and gold ingots,
unworked lapis lazuli and cylinder seals. The find
had been buried in bronze chests carrying the name
of Amenemhat II and reveals the type of materials
Asian rulers exchanged with Egypt's kings.

ONCE MORE DIVIDED

The stability of the 12th Dynasty enabled the Egyptians to extend their power and influence beyond the old borders. The 12th Dynasty came to an end around 1795 BC with the female pharaoh Sebekneferu. For 50 years following the accession of a new dynasty, Egypt remained stable, but soon the old divisions resurfaced and the local rulers again seized power. For the next 100 years (1650–1550 BC) Egypt was divided between three main powers: Kush, Thebes and the new northern kingdom of the Hyksos.

The rulers of foreign lands

The people later known as the Hyksos, from the Egyptian term 'ruler of foreign lands', were of Asiatic origin, but many had been settled in Egypt for several generations. The appearance of Hyksos rulers in the eastern part of the Nile Delta does not indicate a foreign conquest. It is more likely that locally powerful men took advantage of the political situation to establish their own rule. These people controlled the routes across Sinai into southern Palestine. They ruled from the city of Avaris in the eastern Delta and adopted the style of Egyptian pharaohs.

Avaris has been the subject of extensive excavations in the past three decades. Among recent discoveries are fragments of painted wall decoration from one of the latest phases of the royal palace at Avaris. These have scenes of bull-jumping that reveal close affinities with Minoan

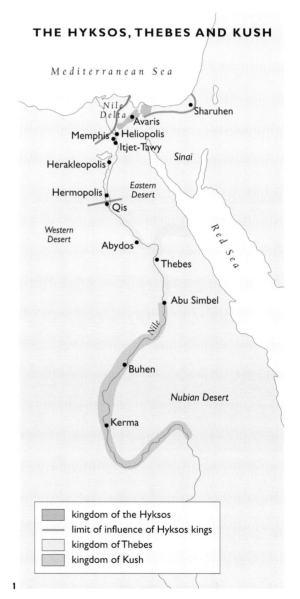

THE HYKSOS, THEBES AND KUSH

1

2

1. From 1650 to 1550 BC Egypt was divided between three main powers: Kush, Thebes and the Hyksos.

2. A fragment of a battle scene of the reign of Menthuhotep II showing defeated opponents, characteristically painted yellow.

There is a total of about 80 royal pyramids in Egypt, including the tombs of kings, queens and princesses. There are also hundreds of smaller mud-brick pyramids built over private tombs.

⭐ If the blocks of stone used to build the Great Pyramid at Giza were sawn into 30-cm (1-ft) cubes, and then placed in a row, they would extend over a distance equal to two-thirds of the Earth's circumference.

Crete. Objects with the names of some of the late Hyksos kings were also found in Crete and Mesopotamia, leading a few earlier archaeologists to suggest that these kings ruled a vast empire. Instead, we now know that the Hyksos kings had wide-ranging trade connections, controlling the African luxury trade. Their trading partner was the kingdom of Kush.

The kingdom of Kush

In Nubia, the Egyptian pharaohs of the 12th Dynasty had supported trade with Kush to the south, and defended the passage through the Second Cataract of the Nile. Now the southern kingdom became so powerful that it was able to drive the Egyptians out of northern Nubia and make itself the ruling power there. The Kushite kings installed their garrisons in the Nubian fortresses originally built by the Egyptians, though many of the commanders were descended from those who had served the pharaohs.

Kerma, the main town in Kush, expanded into a large centre with an enclosed Royal City and high defended wall. During this period, as the rulers of Kush enormously increased their power, so their burial mounds became ever bigger. The last ones were vast tumuli in each of which a ruler was buried surrounded by a great number of his subjects, who were killed to go with him into the afterlife. The wealth and power of Kush were based on trade with the Hyksos rulers, and many clay seals with the names of Hyksos rulers were discovered at Kerma.

1

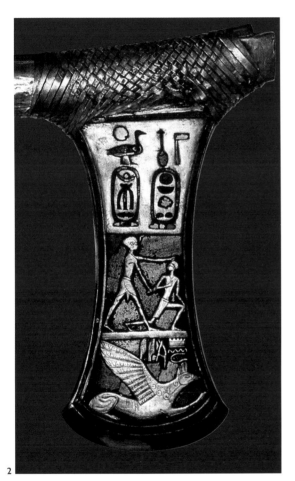

2

Thebes resurgent

The princes of Thebes maintained their rule over southern Egypt from Aswan to Qis. The land was fertile, but the direct contact between Nubia and the Hyksos state in the Nile Delta excluded them from the wealth of foreign trade. Relations with the neighbouring states seem to have been amicable, and the Hyksos kings made dedications in the temples of southern Egypt. There may even have been marriages between the ruling families.

Eventually, the princes of Thebes mustered sufficient strength to challenge the Hyksos. The first to do so, Seqenenre-Tao, was wounded, if not killed, in battle in *c*.1560 BC. His mummy carries gashes caused by axes and spears. His successor, Kamose (*c*.1555-1552 BC), left inscriptions that lament the division of Egypt: 'Why do I bother to contemplate my victories when there is a chief in Avaris and another in Kush, and I am bound to an Asiatic and a Nubian, each man holding his own slice of this Black Land [Egypt] and dividing the country with me?' The inscriptions record his initial attack on Nubia and an assault on the Hyksos. However, the destruction of Avaris and the reunification of Egypt under the New Kingdom did not come until 1550 BC, in the reign of Ahmose I. He marched his army into Nubia, regaining Buhen and the Second Cataract before attacking the north. Driving the Hyksos out of Egypt, he pursued them to the city of Sharuhen in southern Palestine, which was allied with them. The Egyptian expansion into western Asia that followed is often thought of as a response to the Hyksos rule.

1. A pottery vessel in the form of a typical Kushite round house. A wooden frame was covered with thatch, perhaps, like this pot, brightly coloured.

2. The gold and inlay axe of King Ahmose. The god Monthu, who protected the king in battle, is depicted as a griffin.

THE RICHES OF EMPIRE

THE RICHES OF EMPIRE

Between 1550 and 1500 BC, the rulers of Thebes reunited Egypt under their own rule, ushering in the New Kingdom. The new pharaohs soon began to expand the country's borders southwards, far into Nubia, and eastwards into western Asia, where they reached the River Euphrates. Their far-ranging military expeditions extended Egypt's sphere of influence into northern Syria, giving it control of the major trade routes between western Asia and Africa. Egypt had acquired an empire. The Egyptians brought home booty from captured cities and imposed regular payment of tax and tribute on them. One of the most important factors in this new age of empire was the change in warfare brought about by the introduction of chariots and horses from northern Syria. But it was diplomacy and the exchange of valuable goods that maintained Egypt's empire for 200 years.

Previous page: Colossal statues of pharaohs in pink granite flank one of the gateways along the processional route in the temple of Amun at Thebes.

CREATING AN EMPIRE

Chariots added a new dimension to warfare in western Asia. Archaeologists once thought that the appearance of horses and chariots from around 1700 BC indicated the emergence of a new race of warrior rulers across the region. We now know this was not so, and that it was peoples in northern Syria and eastern Anatolia who first developed chariots. Their use spread, though at first in small numbers. An early ruler of the Hittite kingdom in Anatolia had only 80 chariots; by 1274 BC the massed armies of a later Hittite king and his allies had more than 3500 chariots when they confronted the pharaoh Ramesses II at the Battle of Qadesh.

The first chariots in Egypt were those of the Hyksos rulers (▷ p. 42) in the Nile Delta. With the emergence of the New Kingdom after 1550 BC, the warrior pharaohs of a reunited Egypt soon acquired chariots of their own through trade and capture. The seizure of large numbers of chariots and horses is almost invariably detailed in the inscriptions that recount the battles of these pharaohs. In one great encounter, at Megiddo (c.1456 BC), Thutmose III claimed to have taken 924 chariots from the defeated princes of Syria. The Egyptians were soon manufacturing their own chariots, importing the necessary timber, such as ash and birch, from the deciduous forests of Anatolia and even farther north. Horses, too, had

1. Hittite chariots at the Battle of Qadesh (1274 BC). Heavier than those of their Egyptian opponents, the chariots were large enough to carry three men.

to be imported in large numbers. The ability to drive a chariot, as well as the ability to write, became an identifying characteristic of Egypt's ruling élite.

As the chariot's use spread throughout the Near East, it was adapted to the local environment and different types of warfare. Egyptian chariots were lightweight and carried only two men, the charioteer and a warrior. In battle, they were used as firing platforms for archers. The Hittites, who were to become for a while Egypt's principal opponents, developed a much heavier chariot that carried three men, fighting from it with swords and stabbing spears. Another important introduction was the composite bow, developed like the chariot

in northern Syria. This was made of wood, horn and sinew, bonded together, and provided great range and accuracy.

Vying for power

In the period from 1500 to 1200 BC, known as the Late Bronze Age, the chariot helped to create new kingdoms such as that of the Mitanni, whose heartland lay in northern Syria near the River Euphrates. Mitanni held a key strategic position, controlling much of the trade in horses, chariots and timber with the regions beyond it in Anatolia. From its capital city, Washshukanni, it dominated a host of satellite kingdoms, such as Aleppo, and

1. Tutankhamun charges the enemy in a light Egyptian chariot. The king is shown with the reins tied around his waist, although in reality he would have been driven.

2. During the New Kingdom, powerful states, such as Hatti and Mitanni, vied with Egypt for control of Phoenicia, Syria and Canaan.

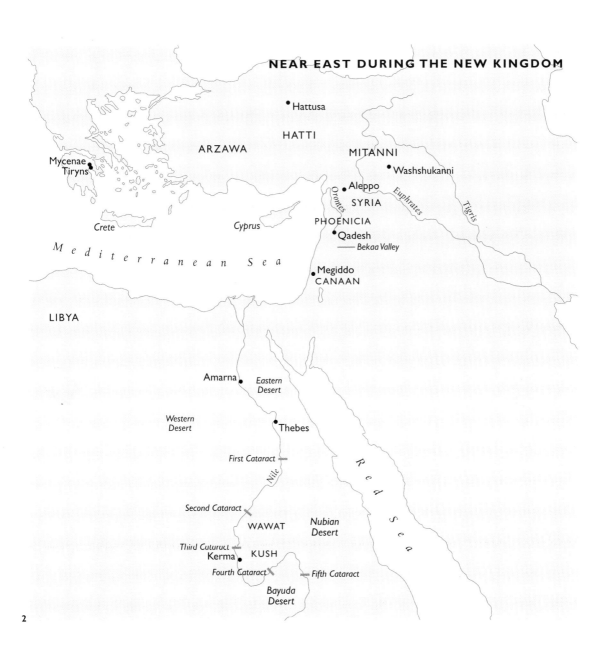

NEAR EAST DURING THE NEW KINGDOM

Hattusa

HATTI

ARZAWA

MITANNI

Washshukanni

Mycenae
Tiryns

Aleppo

Orontes

Euphrates

SYRIA

Tigris

Crete

Cyprus

PHOENICIA

Qadesh

Bekaa Valley

M e d i t e r r a n e a n   S e a

Megiddo

CANAAN

LIBYA

Amarna

*Eastern
Desert*

*Western
Desert*

Thebes

First Cataract

Nile

R e d   S e a

Second Cataract

WAWAT

*Nubian
Desert*

Third Cataract

Kerma

KUSH

Fourth Cataract

Fifth Cataract

*Bayuda
Desert*

2

1

 THE EGYPTIAN TEMPLE

The pharaohs of the New Kingdom built massive temples to the state gods of Egypt. The most splendid surviving temple is the great temple of Amun at Thebes (modern Karnak). These vast complexes served as state treasuries, schools and workshops. The wealth of empire was brought to the workshops to be turned into a vast array of luxury goods, which were sent by the pharaohs as gifts to their 'brother' kings and to their officials. As the New Kingdom pharaohs were buried in rock-cut tombs (such as those in the Valley of the Kings) that could be created by a relatively small number of highly skilled artisans, temples replaced pyramids as the major projects of state labour. Although much of the stone for the temples was quarried locally, limestone and sandstone, as well as blocks of granite and quartzite for statuary, were brought from farther away during the flood season.

1. The temple of Amun at Thebes was one of the most spectacular buildings of the New Kingdom. Massive towers originally flanked the gateway.

extended northwest into Anatolia. Further west, in the heart of Anatolia, the kingdom of Hatti (the Hittites) became the major state. In southern Mesopotamia, Babylon was the dominant power under the rule of the Kassite dynasty (c.1530–1155 BC), but towards the end of the Late Bronze Age, the northern Mesopotamian kingdom of Assyria began to make its mark. These large, powerful states all vied with Egypt for control of the city-states of Phoenicia, Syria and Canaan. The Egyptians, meanwhile, were expanding their own empire not only into Asia, but also southwards along the Nile Valley into the region of Nubia and beyond.

Conquering Kush

Altogether it took the New Kingdom rulers a hundred years to impose their rule over the whole of Nubia as far south as the Fourth Cataract of the Nile. The first phase was essentially defensive. Kamose, the last Theban king before the reunification of Egypt, and his successor Ahmose (1552–1527 BC), founder of the New Kingdom, led their armies into Nubia in order to regain control of the fortresses of the Second Cataract (▷ p. 38). Their aim was to protect their southern frontier against attack by the kingdom of Kush (southern

2. The people of western Asia are shown wearing typical costume and with characteristic pointed beards. They are bringing tribute to the Egyptian court, which includes elaborate metal vessels made of silver and gold.

Nubia), before embarking on their wars against the Hyksos. But Kush remained a threat, and Thutmose I (1504–1492 BC) led a major Egyptian offensive to crush its power. Excavation at Kerma has shown that there was massive destruction by fire in the city. Despite this, Kerma was soon rebuilt and the Kushites continued to put up powerful opposition to Egyptian ambitions for another 30 years at least.

Southern Nubia was finally brought under Egyptian rule during the joint reign of Thutmose III (1479–1425 BC) and Hatshepsut (1472–1458 BC). Thutmose III had ascended the throne as a child and, for the first 20 years of his reign, Hatshepsut, his father's chief wife, acted as regent and then joint pharaoh. Thutmose commanded some of the expeditions into Nubia, but the first may have been led by Hatshepsut herself. Once Thutmose had established his sway over the local Kushite princes

★ For religious reasons, the Egyptian pharaoh was male by definition. When Hatshepsut became pharaoh, she was depicted in sculptures as a man, with the royal beard and kilt, and a male physique.

1

2

1. Thutmose III (1479–1425 BC) wears the royal headcloth, the nemes. Less remote than the pharaohs of the Old Kingdom and more idealized than those of the Middle Kingdom, the statue is typical of the New Kingdom.

2. A glazed tile depicting a Kushite prince. He wears a large gold earring. Kushite princes were shown in a costume that combined an Egyptian robe with their traditional insignia.

as far south as the Fourth Cataract of the Nile, he took his army farther south, into the savannas of Sudan. This was not territory he intended to conquer; he simply wanted to show his might to discourage attacks on his empire's new southern frontier.

The Egyptians imposed a new administration on Nubia. This included some officials from Egypt, but it was largely in the hands of the local élites. The officials included Kushite princes, a chief of the militia and, most important of all, an Egyptian viceroy. Called the King's Son of Kush, the viceroy was responsible for collecting taxes and tribute in the country. The gold-mining regions of the Eastern Desert were now exploited intensively; gold became the principal product of Wawat (northern Nubia). The south, Kush, offered the wealth of long-distance trade: ivory, ebony, incense, animal skins and live animals. Also important were the local products of the Nile Valley, notably dates and cattle. Slaves, too, were sent to Egypt. These were usually people captured by the rulers of the south. They were not used as agricultural labourers, but served in palaces, temples or the army. The wealth that poured into Egypt from Nubia played a vital role in establishing the pharaohs' international position.

From the Nile to the Euphrates

Having made sure that his more vulnerable southern border was protected, Thutmose III turned his attention to the east. Before him, Amenhotep I (1527–1506 BC) had marched his armies through Asia, and Thutmose I (1504–1492) had reached the River Euphrates, where he left an inscription. As in Nubia, the kings took their armies beyond the limit they intended to absorb, as a show of strength. Both earlier pharaohs had made Egypt's ambitions in western Asia obvious and gained the recognition of local rulers, but it was Thutmose III who really established the empire.

The dominant power in western Asia and Egypt's principal rival was the kingdom of Mitanni. Following the death of Hatshepsut, Thutmose III took his armies into Asia nearly every year for 20 years. There were many minor skirmishes and a couple of major battles, the most significant being at Megiddo in about 1456 BC, where Thutmose

triumphed over a coalition of Syrian princes. As a result of these campaigns, Egypt and Mitanni established their respective spheres of influence, Egypt dominating the coast of Phoenicia as far north as the mouth of the Orontes river.

The Egyptians imposed garrisons and an administration in western Asia along much the same lines as they had done in Nubia. Egyptian control of the southern regions of Canaan was fairly secure, but the rulers of northern cities, most notably Qadesh, frequently abandoned their loyalty to Egypt when threatened by the armies of either Mitanni or Hatti.

1

'SEND ME MORE GOLD!'

Thutmose III established the limits of Egypt's empire in Asia and Africa. The reigns of his successors saw diplomacy replace war as a means of maintaining empires. Frequent letters and gifts were exchanged between a network of rulers stretching from Babylonia and Assyria in Mesopotamia to the Hittites and the kingdom of Arzawa in western Anatolia. Marriages may well have sealed the relationship between kings – but even more important than this was the exchange of gold between them.

Ruling an empire

Egypt's new empire brought changes within the country itself. The acquisition of new territories required the appointment of many more scribes and administrators, and consequently there was an increase in the size of the bureaucracy. In the Old and Middle Kingdoms, the same officials had performed a variety of tasks, but now the complexity of running an empire meant a much more specialized administration was needed.

A scribal élite was educated in the temple and palace schools, where from an early age boys learnt how to write, then from about the age of seven, they were also trained in the art of chariotry. This education may have been followed by military service in the chariot corps before they took up positions in one of the branches of the administration: the priesthood, the civil service or the army. Even though there were many more scribes,

2

1. A typical banqueting scene of the New Kingdom. The married couples, single men and single women all sat in separate groups.

2. A statue of one of Amenhotep III's chief advisors, Amenhotep the son of Hapu, who is shown as a scribe.

the number of top positions was still very small, and competition for those jobs must have been strong. It was common for some of the highest officials, such as the vizier, to have sons and brothers who were simple scribes, or holders of what might be considered lowly offices.

The expansion of the empire also brought many foreigners to Egypt, and this had an impact on Egyptian culture. From the time of Thutmose I, Kushite princes were brought to the Egyptian court to be educated, and returned to their realms as vassals of the pharaoh. Asiatic princes soon joined the Kushites in the palace schools. The foreign princesses who came as wives for pharaohs brought large numbers of attendants and servants.

 HOUSES

For poor people in Egypt, home was small and cramped. Several villages built for the royal artisans have survived: the houses often have only one bedroom for the head of the household and his wife. The houses of officials, by contrast, were large compounds enclosed by walls, and consisting of the main residence, servants' quarters and storage areas. Where space allowed, these houses were single-storey villas, but in the cities they were on several levels, usually with the kitchen on the roof. For rich and poor alike, interiors were dark, with a few small windows placed high in the walls to keep out the hot sun. Ceilings were blackened by lamp smoke.

1

There is good evidence that Syrians, Nubians, Libyans and people from Anatolia were in the service of the pharaohs, both in the palace and the administration. In one tomb scene from the reign of Akhenaten (1352–1336 BC), Syrian musicians are shown playing while the king and his family enjoy their dinner. Some foreign attendants took Egyptian names, thus honouring the pharaoh whom they served: Heqa-nefer, 'the good ruler', or Menkheperre-seneb, 'may Thutmose III be healthy'! Later, many foreign mercenary soldiers came to join the army and were given grants of land when their service was over.

The international age

The complex international relations of the Late Bronze Age are documented by a large archive of letters found at the site of Amarna, in the ancient city of Akhetaten built by the pharaoh Akhenaten in about 1350 BC. The surviving archive, only a fragment of the original, contains copies of letters between the Egyptian court and its vassals and allies in Cyprus, Syria, Mitanni, Assyria and Babylon. The letters were written on clay tablets, using the cuneiform script of wedge-shaped strokes stamped into clay that had been originally devised in Mesopotamia.

The principal correspondence in the Amarna archive is between Egypt and Mitanni. It is particularly detailed about the arrangements and protocol of royal marriages. The pharaohs Thutmose IV, Amenhotep III and Akhenaten all married daughters of the kings of Mitanni. When

2

1. The Nubian prince Maiherpri, here shown on his funerary papyrus, was raised at the Egyptian court, but died aged about 20.

2. Tutankhamun's mask shows the technical skill of the Egyptian goldsmith. It is beaten from two sheets of gold and inlaid with glass and semi-precious stones.

the king of either Mitanni or Egypt died, a new alliance had to be made between the countries. So when Shuttarna of Mitanni died, Amenhotep III (1390–1352 BC), who was already married to one of Shuttarna's daughters, had to take one of the new king's daughters as a wife as well. Letters detail the huge dowry of the princess, which included quantities of jewellery, clothing and furniture, but also chariots and other military equipment.

Every time a letter was sent from one ruler to another it was accompanied by a gift, and each gift had to be equal to that received: some kings complain that their gifts have not been matched. The gift most sought after was gold. Some rulers write to the pharaoh that 'Gold is like dirt in Egypt, you can simply pick it up!'; whereas others

complain about the quality of the gold they have been sent. Many of them simply write: 'Send me more gold!'

Trading in gifts

The pharaoh controlled all foreign trade, which operated through the exchange of 'gifts'. Egypt sent the wealth it received from Kush to foreign rulers and received similar things in return. Valuable timber, such as cedar and pine from Lebanon and Syria, or ash and birch from Mitanni, was essential for chariot and bow-making, and was exchanged for gold, ivory and ebony. Lapis lazuli was brought from Afghanistan and became one of the most important items of exchange offered by the

 AKHENATEN

One of the most intriguing pharaohs is Akhenaten (see right), who introduced an extravagant, mannered style of art, and focused religion on the worship of the sun. His reign lasted for 17 years, from 1352 to 1336 BC, at the height of the Egyptian empire. Earlier Egyptologists thought of him as a peace-loving ruler whose religion was an early form of monotheism, and whose hymns to the sun influenced the Psalms of David. Now, however, he is regarded more as a reactionary who was trying to emulate the remote god-kings of the pyramid age. His reign saw the creation of a new royal city, Akhetaten, 'The Horizon of the Sun-Disk' (modern Amarna). This was abandoned after his death. Its temples were pulled down and the stone was recycled in other buildings.

1. A smith at work, with pincers and pipe to direct the heat. His three-legged stool ensured stability on an uneven earth floor.

Babylonians. Metals, such as copper, came from Cyprus and Asia. Horses were brought from Syria, wine and olive oil from Canaan, the region between the Mediterranean and the Dead Sea.

There is also evidence of Egypt's contacts across the Mediterranean with the Mycenaeans in Greece and the Minoans in Crete. Besides raw materials, the products of the royal workshops were sent. The Amarna letters describe in great detail pieces of furniture with their decorations, the types of wood used and overlays of sheet gold.

The giving of gifts was important within Egypt, too: the pharaoh gave gold to his officials as a reward. In the scenes from tombs that show the rewarding of officials, we always see three or four scribes taking account of the amounts of each item distributed. In this way, the officials enjoyed the wealth of empire, which was carefully allocated according to rank. The officials themselves probably passed on some of their reward to their subordinates, so wealth filtered downward, though it did not reach the Egyptian agricultural labourers.

1

CRISIS IN THE EMPIRES

For a hundred years until about 1350 BC, there was peace among the great empires of western Asia. But in the reign of Akhenaten and his successors, Tutankhamun (1336–1327 BC) and Horemheb (1327–1294 BC), a threat to Egypt's empire appeared in the form of the Hittites. Their invasion was the beginning of a series of crises that ultimately saw the collapse of all of the great powers in the region and the start of dramatic changes that reverberated throughout western Asia. Having established control over much of central Anatolia by 1400 BC,

the Hittites expanded their influence eastwards into northern Syria. Here they confronted the kingdom of Mitanni and its allies. The first crisis came during the reign of Akhenaten, when the Hittite king marched into the territory of Mitanni. He sacked the capital and reduced their kings to Hittite vassals. Some territories previously loyal to Egypt, notably Qadesh, went over to the Hittites. The Egyptian army then marched north, peace was restored and Qadesh returned to Egyptian control.

Fifty years late came a more serious conflict, when further Hittite expansion led to war with Egypt in the reigns of Sety I (1294–1279 BC) and

1

Ramesses II (1279–1212 BC). Again, the focus was the important trading city of Qadesh in Syria, strategically sited on the Orontes river and at the end of the fertile Bekaa Valley. The key offensive came in the fifth year (1274 BC) of the reign of Ramesses II, when the Egyptian and Hittite armies met outside the walls of Qadesh. Ramesses considered this battle to be his greatest victory, and reliefs showing it were carved in several temples. But Hittite records of the battle have also survived, from which it is clear that there was no real victor.

A marriage contract

To seal the peace between Egypt and the Hittites, Ramesses II married the daughter of the Hittite king. The event is recorded in a 'marriage stele', a stone slab carved with scenes that commemorate the event. The Hittite princess is shown being taken to Egypt by her father in the 34th year of Ramesses II's reign. The text says that an Egyptian escort went to meet her in Syria. She adopted the rather lengthy Egyptian name, Maet-hor-neferure, 'She who beholds the falcon (the king) that is the visible splendour of Re'. The new queen appeared on official monuments and as a diminutive figure standing at the king's side on a colossal image from the temple of Tanis.

Ramesses devoted his next years to securing control of Canaan and the regions much farther south. The Hittites, meanwhile, were hampered by internal power struggles. During these years,

1. The army, carrying axes and throw sticks, accompany a religious procession.

 WOMEN AND LAW

Although they could hold important religious positions, women in Egypt were not able to hold administrative offices: their prime role was as wives and mothers. Nevertheless, the women of the élite classes could deputize in some capacities during their husbands' absences. They also had more legal rights than most women in the ancient world. Women could inherit and bequeath land and other property, and act on their own behalf in legal transactions. Many legal documents from the Late Period attest women engaged in such business activities. In the Late Period, and perhaps earlier, women could initiate divorce proceedings. Prenuptial agreements ensured that a woman took all her property with her in the event of divorce.

another empire, Assyria, took advantage of the Hittites' problems and absorbed the last fragments of the kingdom of Mitanni.

Danger from the west

For the pharaohs Sety I and Ramesses II, the Libyans posed another threat. They had always been a traditional enemy of Egypt on its Western Desert edge, but suddenly they emerged as a major force to be reckoned with. 'Libyans' is a rather vague term for the people who lived outside the settled Nile Valley and Delta to the west. They were

2

1. (opposite) The entrance gateway with its obelisks and statues was added by Ramesses II to the temple of Amun at Luxor built by Amenhotep III.

2. Shardana mercenary troops engage with the invading Sea Peoples in Egypt's first recorded sea battle.

mostly nomadic or semi-nomadic. There were frequent movements of Libyans along the coast into Egypt, and forts were built on the Mediterranean coast to control them. Ramesses II absorbed many of these people into Egypt, settling them in the eastern Nile Delta.

In the reign of Ramesses II's son, Merenptah (1212–1202 BC), large numbers of Libyans, dominated by the tribe of the Libu, launched an armed invasion of Egypt, where they advanced almost as far as Memphis. They were aided by mercenary troops, who came from a wide range of countries and were usually called the Sea Peoples. The Sea Peoples became even more important some 30 years later, when Ramesses III (1184–1153 BC) faced two major Libyan wars and one against the Sea Peoples. The Libyan invasions in the fifth and eighth years of Ramesses III's reign involved the Libu, but were led by another tribe, the Meshwesh. Other tribal groups took part and altogether the invasion numbered many thousands of people. When forced back, they began to move southwards through the oases of the desert and into Egypt along its vulnerable desert roads, eventually settling down reasonably peacefully.

Warriors from the sea

The Sea Peoples have been blamed for destruction at numerous sites in Greece, the Aegean and around the coast of the eastern Mediterranean. The cities of Mycenae and Tiryns on mainland Greece, Knossos on Crete, and the Hittite capital Hattusa (modern Bodhazkoy) in Anatolia, along with many other ▷▷

important centres, were all destroyed around this time by fires, and many scholars have attributed these catastrophes to attacks by the Sea Peoples.

The Sea Peoples were once thought to be large populations moving as a mass from northern Anatolia along the coast of Phoenicia and Palestine. It was thought that they were then repulsed at the entrance to Egypt and scattered. The names of the different groups among them are preserved in the Egyptian texts recording the conflicts. They were the Shekelesh, Shardana, Ekwesh, Lukka, Teresh, Weshesh, Denyen and Peleset. Long ago, the similarities between these names and a number of

place names around the Mediterranean were recognized. It was assumed that, driven back from Egypt, they settled in the places that later carried their names – so the Shekelesh were thought to have gone to Sicily, the Shardana to Sardinia, and the Peleset to have remained in Palestine. Scholars are no longer so sure. One thing, however, is clear: many of these groups were not new in the eastern Mediterranean. Some had been serving as mercenary soldiers in the armies of Egypt, and in those of the Libyans, in the reign of Ramesses II. It seems likely, therefore, that the Sea Peoples were largely mercenary troops, rather than a mass

Previous page: The massive rock-cut temple of Abu Simbel in Nubia is dominated by the four seated colossi of the king.

1. The walls of the temples are covered with inscriptions and reliefs attesting the pharaoh's devotion to the gods.

2. Ram-headed sphinxes, images of the god Amun, flanked the processional way to the temple dedicated to him at Thebes.

1

2

movement of displaced peoples. But this does not
alter the fact that from around 1200 BC the great
empires of the Late Bronze Age began to collapse
and fragment. There certainly were movements of
population, but it is at least as likely that these were
caused by political change as that they provoked
the change in the first place.

Climate, too, may possibly have had an effect.
There have been numerous attempts to identify
major changes in weather patterns as revealed by
tree rings, but no convincing climatic cause has yet
been proved. Famine certainly lay behind the
Libyan migrations, but there is no evidence of
similar problems in Egypt itself, and the Libyan
famine may have been a localized crisis.

★ The Egyptians shaved their
heads, or had very close-
cut hair. They wore elaborate
ringleted wigs that were made of
human hair and vegetable fibres
such as flax or grass.

EGYPT AND THE NEW EMPIRES

EGYPT AND THE NEW EMPIRES

The old empires of western Asia were fast crumbling; Egypt was in decline. By 1200 BC, the political map of western Asia was changing dramatically. The archaeological evidence from many regions becomes sparse and confusing, and this has led to the period between 1200 and 900 BC being called a 'dark age'. It was a time of turmoil, in which the previous empires were replaced by smaller kingdoms. Although less seriously affected than other regions, even Egypt suffered from political division. From 900 BC onwards, new empires arose in Mesopotamia and Persia. The first was the Assyrian empire, which extended its boundaries to the Mediterranean and then towards Egypt. But it was another new power in Africa – Kush – that first conquered Egypt. From 665 BC Egypt's rulers tried to re-establish the old influence, with varying success, before falling first to the Persians and finally to the Macedonians.

RISING NEW POWERS

Ramesses III is usually held up as the last of the great warrior pharaohs, while his successors are dismissed as ineffectual rulers presiding over Egypt's inglorious decline. In fact, Egypt retained its empire in western Asia until the reign of Ramesses VI (1143–1136 BC), when there are signs of major destruction in its Asian garrisons and administrative centres. In Nubia the crisis came later, probably in the reign of Ramesses XI (1099–1069 BC), and it seems to have been very sudden. The Egyptians abandoned the administrative towns of Kush, and their southern frontier was redrawn at the Second Cataract of the Nile. The end of Ramesses XI's reign saw power struggles and civil war in Egypt. The Egyptians lost their remaining hold on Nubia, and the southern frontier was once more redrawn, this time at Aswan. In 1069 BC, a new dynasty, the 21st, came to power, under which Egypt was effectively divided: the kings of the 21st Dynasty ruled from the city of Tanis in the eastern Nile Delta, but their relatives, serving as the High Priests of Amun, were in control of much of the Nile Valley.

Israel, Judah and Damascus

By 1200 BC, Egypt was in relative eclipse and the kingdoms of the Hittites and Mitanni had collapsed. For the first time in generations, the peoples of Syria and Palestine were no longer subservient to empires from outside their region. In the end, power moved into the region with the appearance of a new kingdom, Israel.

For three generations from around 1020 BC, Israel under kings Saul, David and Solomon was the most powerful trading kingdom in western Asia. But after the death of Solomon around 931 BC, the kingdom split in two: the northern kingdom, Israel, was ruled from the new capital of Samaria; the southern kingdom, Judah, from Jerusalem. Despite

1. A Phoenician ivory plaque in Egyptian style with a cartouche carrying a non-Egyptian name, perhaps *Lau-bidi.*

their close religious and political ties, Israel and Judah were sometimes allies and sometimes enemies. A short way to the east, across the River Jordan, lay their chief rival, the kingdom of Damascus. These three were surrounded by other small kingdoms. In the north, the successors of the Hittite kingdom and Mitanni were scattered throughout Syria. Along the coast, the old trading cities of Phoenicia, such as Byblos and Tyre (▷ p. 83), enjoyed great prosperity.

The Phoenician cities now began to send their ships farther and farther afield in search of precious metals, notably silver and tin. They also began to found colonies, first in Cyprus and then along the North African coast as far as Spain. The most famous, and ultimately the most powerful, of these was Carthage (in modern Tunisia).

Egypt's cultural influence

Although Egypt no longer had an empire, its trade with the Phoenicians and its cultural influence on their cities appears to have been particularly strong at this time. Fine-quality linen was exported from Egypt to cities such as Tyre, where it was coloured purple using the local mollusc, murex, as a dye. Another increasingly important Egyptian export was papyrus. Aramaic, the native language of the Aramaean peoples originally of northern Syria, was rapidly replacing Akkadian as the international tongue, and was written in an alphabetic script in ink on papyrus rolls, rather than with a stylus on clay tablets. As the use of Aramaic spread, so did the demand for Egyptian papyrus.

1

1. The only known representation of an Israelite king comes from the 9th century BC. By then the kingdoms in Syria and Palestine faced a mortal threat from the expanding Assyrian empire. Here, an Assyrian relief shows Jehu, king of Israel, abjectly kissing the ground before Shalmaneser III of Assyria (858–824 BC) as he pays tribute to the Assyrian monarch.

1

 SIEGE AND DEPORTATION

The Assyrian army was the most formidable fighting machine of the 7th century BC. Equipped with siege engines, scaling ladders, towers and equipment to undermine walls, the Assyrians could launch an assault that few cities in western Asia were strong enough to resist. When they captured a city, the Assyrians frequently deported some of its population to Assyria. The deportees were often members of the ruling élite, or highly skilled workers. Occasionally, the Assyrians meted out harsh justice on rebels, impaling them on stakes outside the city walls as a warning to others.

1. Deportation was frequently practised by the Assyrians. It was a means of preventing rebellion, and supplied skilled artisans to the empire.

2. The treasures from conquered cities were taken to Assyria, where some of the ivory furniture has been discovered in excavations.

2

Egyptian influence on the Phoenician cities in this period is also strikingly evident in the decorative arts, notably in elaborately carved ivory panels, many used for thrones and chairs. The ivory itself probably came from Nubia or Ethiopia, either through Egypt or along Red Sea routes. The ivories have survived because they were looted and taken as trophies to the royal palaces of a fast-rising power in western Asia – the Assyrian empire.

Assyria

For 200 years, beginning in the 9th century BC, Assyria was the region's dominant state. Its advantage was military. The Assyrians continued to use heavy chariots, similar to the Hittite model, but they also increasingly deployed cavalry. This was made possible by the introduction of larger breeds of horse from northern Iran. The Assyrian army also had iron weapons. Even more important, probably, was the army itself, which the Assyrian king Tiglath-pileser III (744–727BC) moulded into the most efficient fighting machine of its day.

A vigorous and highly astute ruler, Tiglath-pileser had usurped the Assyrian throne in a coup against his brother Ashur-nirari V. He reformed the administration of the country, introduced conscription for the army, and then set about bringing the neighbouring peoples of Mesopotamia firmly under Assyrian control. Next he turned his attention westwards. At first, his aim and that of his successors was to extend Assyria's influence over Syria and the coastal cities in order to gain their wealth through trade and tribute. In the ▷▷

Previous page: The people of Lachish in Judah being sent into captivity in Assyria. The Assyrians stormed the city in 701 BC, but failed to take Judah's capital, Jerusalem.

1. This scene from the funerary papyrus of Khonsumose typifies the elegance of Egyptian art of the Libyan period.

2. The gold funerary mask of Psusennes I from the royal tombs at Tanis.

1

south, Israel, Judah and Damascus survived as kingdoms, though under Assyrian overlordship, until constant rebellion saw many such kingdoms reduced to provinces. By 720 BC, only Judah was left of the kingdoms in the south. The Assyrian empire now stretched from the Egyptian border in the southwest, north into Anatolia and east as far as the Persian Gulf and into western Iran.

Libyan pharaohs

In Egypt, meanwhile, Libyan military leaders, descended from the groups that had settled in the country under the 20th Dynasty, had established a ruling dynasty of their own – the 22nd. Its founder was Sheshonq I. A dynamic figure, Sheshonq succeeded his uncle, usually known as Osorkon the Elder. Although he managed to gain control of the whole of Egypt, and was acknowledged as pharaoh in the north, Sheshonq was still known at Thebes for some years by his Libyan title, Great Chief of the Meshwesh.

The Libyan pharaohs of the 22nd Dynasty ruled from Tanis and Bubastis, both in the eastern Nile Delta, and also from the ancient city of Memphis. Tanis lay near the eastern frontier of Egypt, and Sheshonq tried to reassert Egyptian authority across the southern kingdoms of Asia. He left a large inscription in the temple of Amun at Thebes detailing his capture of cities in Palestine and raids into the kingdom of Israel. Apart from this, there is little evidence of large-scale military activities by the Libyan kings. There are no signs, for example, that they made any attempt to regain Nubia.

2

Our understanding of the period of Libyan rule is coloured by the surviving evidence and the limits of archaeology. The Libyan kings were buried in the Nile Delta cities, rather than in Thebes as their predecessors had been, and most of their building work was concentrated in the Delta. There has been much less excavation in the cities of the Nile Delta than at sites farther south, although this is now changing. Nonetheless, many coffins and funerary materials do survive from this period, and these reveal significant changes in burial customs. People no longer built the tomb chapels that had been typical of the earlier periods. Instead, bodies were buried in large groups, often in earlier tombs. Coffins became elaborate, adorned with the kinds of religious scene formerly found on the walls of tomb chapels.

Mummification reached its most elaborate form during this period. The face and body were packed to give them a more lifelike appearance, and the mummy was covered with protective amulets. Among amulets commonly found on mummies are the scarab, the eye of Horus, the girdle of Isis, and small figures of deities and sacred animals. Instead of the household objects that have been found in earlier tombs, only a few religious objects were buried with the mummy. These include funerary papyri, which were inscribed with all or parts of various religious books, such as the *Book of the Dead*, to guide the dead through the underworld and the various transformations that took place there. As a result, the skills of the artist were concentrated on painting coffins and papyri, and many beautiful examples of draughtsmanship survive.

RULERS FROM THE SOUTH

By the time the Egyptians had abandoned southern Nubia in the reign of Ramesses XI (1099–1069 BC), the territory as a whole was no longer the asset it once had been. The gold mines of northern Nubia had been almost completely exhausted for the past hundred years; the region had become a drain on Egypt's resources rather than a source of its wealth.

Evidence that survives from the period of three centuries following the end of the 20th Dynasty in 1069 BC suggests that there were periods of civil war, with rival local rulers and families competing for power. The ultimate victors were chiefs who lived near the Fourth Cataract of the Nile. Their territory controlled the routes across the Bayuda Desert, south of the Nile, to the savanna of central Sudan. How these rulers increased their wealth and military power remains unclear, but by the middle of the 8th century BC one of them, Kashta, had gained sufficient power in Nubia to take his armies north into Egypt – to Aswan and then Thebes. Kashta was recognized as king in Thebes and southern Egypt and seems to have placed military garrisons in the chief towns.

1

1. The Assyrian army storms an Egyptian city with its Kushite garrison.

2. By 720 BC the Assyrian empire stretched from Anatolia in the north to the Persian Gulf in the east, and southwest to the Egyptian border.

Rival kingdoms

Kashta died in 747 BC. His successor as king in Nubia was Piye (the name used to be written Piankhy), and he, too, was acknowledged as king in Thebes and southern Egypt. The north, mean-while, had become divided among many rulers. Immediately to the north of Piye's kingdom, there

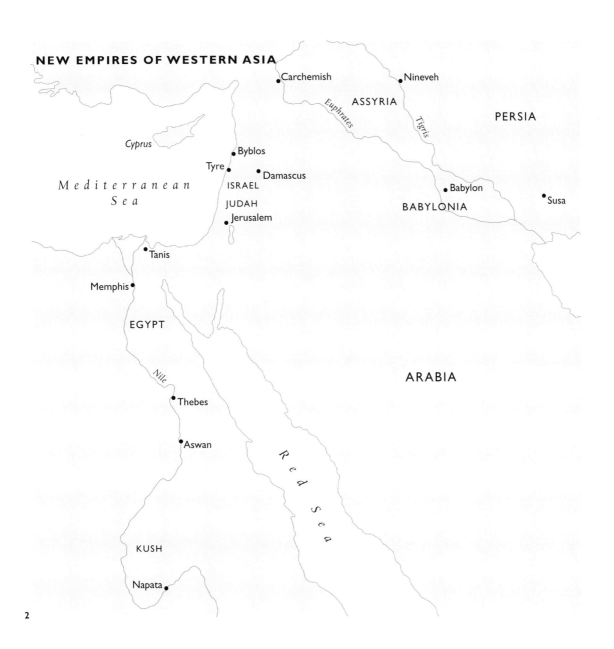

NEW EMPIRES OF WESTERN ASIA

• Carchemish
• Nineveh

ASSYRIA

Euphrates

Tigris

PERSIA

Cyprus

• Byblos
Tyre •
• Damascus

ISRAEL

JUDAH
• Jerusalem

• Babylon

BABYLONIA

• Susa

*Mediterranean
Sea*

• Tanis

Memphis •

EGYPT

Nile

ARABIA

• Thebes

• Aswan

*Red
Sea*

KUSH

Napata •

2

were kings at Hermopolis and Herakleopolis, controlling the rich lands of central Egypt. In the Delta, there were two more kings and a number of Libyan princes. One of these princes, ruling in the western Delta city of Sais, began to gain territory and was soon marching his army southwards into central Egypt. The next 80 years were marked by intermittent conflict between the princes of Sais and the Kushites for control of Egypt.

In the end, the Kushites prevailed, and Piye's successor, Shabaqo (711–695 BC), established himself as pharaoh over the whole of Egypt, acknowledged as overlord by the Libyan chieftains. This new Kushite kingdom was the largest ever seen in the Nile Valley, stretching from the Mediterranean southwards at least as far as present-day Khartoum, at the confluence of the Blue Nile and White Nile.

Kushite rule brought prosperity at home, while abroad the kings soon became involved in the politics of western Asia, where they supported the local rulers, notably the kings of Judah, against the aggression of Assyria. The eventual result of this policy was direct conflict. The Assyrians led three campaigns into Egypt, in which they captured and sacked both Memphis and Thebes. The Kushite pharaoh Taharqo (690–664 BC) put up strong resistance to the Assyrians, but was weakened by the self-interest of the Libyan princes, who continually changed their allegiance.

Taharqo's successor, Tanwetamani (664–656 BC), regained control of Memphis following another Assyrian invasion, but by now a greater threat came from Psamtik, the prince of Sais. Still claiming to be an Assyrian ally, Psamtik managed

 WIVES OF GOD

From 1000 to 600 BC, one of the most important religious offices in Egypt was that of 'God's Wife of Amun'. She was High Priestess and consort of the principal god of Thebes, Amun. There was only one God's Wife, but she adopted her successor who held the office 'Adorer of the God'. The God's Wives were all daughters of kings and presided over a college of priestesses who officiated in the temple. Through various rites they ensured the rebirth of the god every day. The office held vast estates and became economically and politically significant. It was used by the Kushite and Saite kings to ensure that their rule was acknowledged in Thebes.

1. The ibis was associated with Thoth, the god of writing and wisdom.

to take control of the northern part of Egypt and establish himself as king. The Kushites redrew the northern boundary of their realm in central Egypt, but nine years later Psamtik's power had grown so much that he was able to take Thebes and southern Egypt. The Kushite armies withdrew into Nubia, and Egypt was reunited again under one king.

Renaissance

The rule of the Kushite and Saite kings was a time of major building works throughout Egypt and Nubia. Thebes briefly regained some its old importance and received royal endowments. The sculpture of the Late Period was modelled on the great works of the past, resulting in a distinctive style and works that technically equalled those of

the earlier periods. In literature and religion, too, there were important developments. From this time onwards animal cults became particularly popular. Animals that represented a particular god were mummified and offered at special temples by pilgrims. With another change in funerary customs, tomb chapels were once again being built. Now many of them were on a massive scale, some larger even than the royal tombs of Egypt's imperial age. They were lavishly decorated with relief sculpture, mostly religious, but sometimes copying the daily life scenes from earlier tombs. Another new development was the 'demotic' script, a simplified, highly stylized form of the traditional hieroglyphics, used for hand-written bureaucratic and literary documents. Traditional hieroglyphics continued in use for formal sculpted texts.

Last attempt at empire

Psamtik I reigned for 54 years (664–610 BC). He was able to reunite the country and re-establish the authority of the pharaoh. But his ambitions went further than that: he wanted to restore Egypt's position in western Asia. To help him to achieve this, he employed mercenary troops from Anatolia – from Caria, on the southern Anatolian coast, and later from the Ionian Greek cities of Anatolia's western coast. The Assyrians, meanwhile, were preoccupied with both internal problems and the rising power of their old rival, Babylon, now under a new dynasty.

In 612 BC, the Babylonians under Nabopolassar and allied with the Medes of western Iran, sacked the Assyrian capital of Nineveh. For the Egyptians, it fell to Psamtik I's successor, Nekau II (610–595 BC),

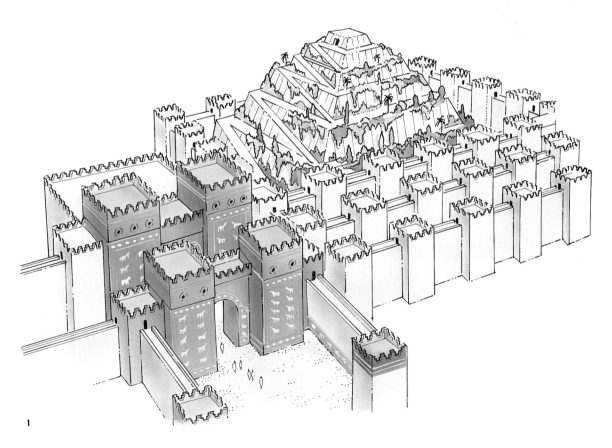

1

1. The city of Babylon was lavishly rebuilt by Nebuchadnezzar, its gates and processional way decorated with blue-glazed brickwork with moulded images.

2. The snake-dragon (mush-hushu) was the symbol of Marduk, the national god of Babylon, and one of the images that appeared on the city's Ishtar Gate.

2

to seek to exploit this situation in a final attempt to regain his kingdom's influence in the region. As champions of the exiled Assyrian king, Egyptian armies once again marched northwards through Asia. Nekau engaged and defeated the king of Judah at Megiddo, and installed his own nominee on the throne. Later, his armies reached the Euphrates where they confronted the Babylonians, led by the crown prince, Nebuchadnezzar. In the event, the Egyptians were defeated, and for the rest of his reign Nekau had to fend off Babylonian attempts to take Egypt. Nebuchadnezzar went on to besiege and sack Jerusalem, bringing the kingdom of Judah to an end. Many Jews were deported to Babylon, while others fled to Egypt.

Ancient Egyptian tomb paintings show that baboons were trained to climb into fig trees and pick the figs, throwing them down to the labourers below.

1. In this Roman relief, the goddess Isis wears the Egyptian crown of horns and disk, and her infant son Horus the double crown, but the style of sculpture is Classical, not Egyptian.

1

Nekau II had more success at sea, where he was responsible for developing Egypt's naval ambitions. He reputedly commissioned a Phoenician fleet to undertake the first circumnavigation of Africa, sailing westwards and returning by the Red Sea. To connect the Nile with the Red Sea, he began building a canal – completed, or enlarged, by the Persian king, Darius I (521–486 BC).

Nekau's successor, Psamtik II (595–589 BC), began his short reign with a major invasion of Nubia, employing mercenary troops from Caria and the Ionian coast. These men left their names and places of origin carved on one of the colossal statues of Ramesses II at Abu Simbel in Nubia and also, a little farther south, in the now-ruined fortress of Buhen. Psamtik II's army fought a battle with the Kushites and may have sacked the city of Napata and the temple of Amun at Gebel Barkal.

Egypt and the Greek world

In the reign of Psamtik I, Greek settlers established colonies in Libya. The most important was at Cyrene, which rapidly developed close contacts with Egypt. In Egypt itself, Greek traders built a base at Naukratis, close to Sais; the archaeological evidence suggests that it was founded in around 620 BC. Egypt's contacts with the Greek world now increased. At first they were with Anatolia's Ionian coast and with Cyrenaica, the Aegean islands and Cyprus; later the mainland cities became important.

Ahmose II (570–526 BC) continued the naval ambitions of Nekau II and managed to gain control of Cyprus, which gave him a base close to the north

 ISIS, A UNIVERSAL GODDESS

In the classical period of ancient Greece and Rome the worship of Isis, Egypt's most important goddess (pictured below), spread throughout the Mediterranean. Temples were built to Isis in numerous cities of the east, North Africa and Italy: the largest and most impressive was in Rome. It was adorned with statuary and obelisks brought from Egypt. The cult of Isis became one of the great mystery religions, with initiation rites that promised hope of salvation and rebirth in the afterlife. As a goddess of fertility, Isis acquired the attributes of the Greek goddess Ceres, and her most potent image was as a mother suckling her baby son, Horus.

Syrian coast. He also established close relations with Polykrates, the ruler of the Greek island of Samos, who supplied him with troops. Ahmose, however, was unable to reassert Egyptian control over western Asia, where yet another new power from the east was poised to conquer.

The empire of the Medes had expanded rapidly since their joint sacking of Nineveh with the Babylonians in 612 BC. While Babylon had taken Syria and Palestine as far as the borders of Egypt, the Median kings had absorbed lands to the north, pushing into central Anatolia, and eastwards towards India. However, in southwestern Iran another small kingdom was emerging in equally spectacular fashion.

The rise of Persia was due to Cyrus the Great (559–530 BC), who conquered the Median empire in 550 BC and captured Babylon in 539. His successor, Cambyses, attacked Egypt. Massed Persian forces advanced in 525 BC. The country was swiftly captured and became a province of the Persian empire. The next 200 years saw a struggle by Egyptian leaders, to free their country from Persian rule.

⭐ At parties, Egyptian women wore cones of perfumed fat on their heads. The fat melted and ran down over their wigs.

STRUGGLE FOR INDEPENDENCE

Most of the rebellions against Persian rule flared up in the towns of the Nile Delta. Egyptian leaders sought the help of the Greek states, notably Athens, and were aided with soldiers and ships. In return, Egypt supplied Athens and other Greek cities with corn in times of shortage. Finally, in 404 BC, a major rebellion succeeded in throwing off Persian rule. After that, a succession of Delta princes claimed the

1

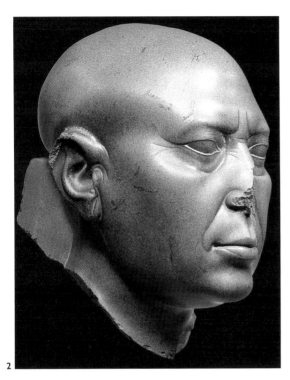

Egyptian throne, until a dynasty of strong rulers asserted itself and ushered in the final period of Egyptian independence. For 40 years from 390 BC, there was a period of relative peace and stability, allowing the first major building works since those of the Saite kings.

The Persians made several attempts to reconquer Egypt, but it was not until 342 BC that they were successful. Even then, another Egyptian prince was able to establish himself as pharaoh for a few years. But the major threat was now not from Persia, but from Macedonia. In 332 BC, Alexander the Great entered Egypt with his army, and the Persian ruler yielded the country without resistance. Alexander took up residence at Memphis before setting off on a long march to the oasis of Siwa. He went along the edge of the Delta to the Mediterranean coast where, at the small port of Rhakote, he founded a new city, named after himself. Alexandria was to become the most important city in the eastern Mediterranean. He then continued along the coast and into the desert. At Siwa Alexander was recognized as son of the god Amun and legitimate pharaoh. He returned to Memphis and established an administration before setting off again on a long march into the heart of the Persian empire.

Partition

Following Alexander's death at Babylon in 323 BC, his empire was partitioned among his generals. Egypt was seized by Ptolemy and the dynasty he founded lasted longer than any of the other new kingdoms. Ptolemy I restored Egypt's position as a

1. Alexander the Great defeated the Persians and initiated 300 years of Greek rule in Egypt.

2. This head in a hard green stone is typical of the superb quality of Late Period sculpture. The features are highly individual, yet stylized.

world power, establishing control, not only over Egypt, but also over the southern part of western Asia as far as Jerusalem and Damascus. To the west he gained Cyrene and the other Greek cities of Libya. Cyprus too became a Ptolemaic possession. Parts of the coast of southern Anatolia, Caria and some of the Ionian towns, along with islands in the Aegean, all entered the Ptolemaic empire.

In Egypt, Ptolemy encouraged Greek settlers and gave land to the veterans of his army. Egypt was generally prosperous, but the benefit was felt mainly by the Greek settlers and the Egyptian élite. The later Ptolemaic period was marred by dynastic conflict in which members of the ruling family began to seek the support of the expanding power of Rome. This culminated in Egypt's involvement in the Roman Civil War (51–30 BC). The defeat of Cleopatra and her lover, the Roman general Antony, saw Egypt absorbed into the Roman Empire.

The Ptolemies encouraged the arts and scholarship, turning Alexandria into one of the greatest centres of Hellenistic culture and learning. Some of

1. The huge Kiosk of the Roman emperor Trajan formed an entrance to the island sanctuary of Isis on the Nubian frontier.

2. With her reputed beauty and tragic end, Egypt's last queen, Cleopatra VII, has inspired dramas of stage and screen – including the Hollywood blockbuster *Cleopatra* (1963), starring Elizabeth Taylor as Cleopatra and Richard Burton as Antony.

3. This shroud clearly shows the mixed culture of Roman Egypt and the continuance of Egyptian religion and customs under domination by Rome.

2

the largest surviving Egyptian temples were also built at this time. In them the Ptolemies, depicted as pharaohs, continued to perform traditional rituals for the Egyptian gods. Hieroglyphic texts continued to be carved on temple walls far into the Roman period, until the 4th century AD. But it was in religion that the cultural influence of Egypt was most strongly felt by the new empire. The worship of Isis and her attendant gods spread throughout the Roman world, becoming one of its most important cults.

3

⭐ The archive of a village scribe, dating from around 250–200 BC, was discovered in 1900. The papyrus rolls, some more than 4 m (13 ft) long, had been used to wrap the mummified sacred crocodiles of the local temple.

FURTHER INFORMATION

BOOKS

Peter A. Clayton, *Chronicle of the Pharaohs* (Thames and Hudson, 1994)
Useful and well-illustrated outline of the history of Egypt for the general reader.

Barry J Kemp, *Ancient Egypt, Anatomy of a Civilization* (Routledge, 1991)
One of the best recent textbooks on Egypt.

Amélie, Kuhrt, *The Ancient Near East c.3000-330 BC* (Routledge, 1995, 2 vols)
The most up-to-date and comprehensive account of the whole of the ancient Near East.

Bill Manley, *The Penguin Historical Atlas of Ancient Egypt* (Penguin Books, 1996)
An outline of Egyptian history well illustrated with maps.

A. Jeffrey Spencer and Stephen Quirke (eds), *The British Museum Book of Ancient Egypt* (British Museum Press, 1992)
A clear introduction to the subject for the general reader.

MAGAZINES

Egyptian Archaeology
The Bulletin of the Egypt Exploration Society. Published twice a year. Contains information on current excavations, exhibitions, books.

KMT, a modern journal of Ancient Egypt
US magazine readily available in the UK, dealing with current issues, exhibitions and new books.

WEBSITES

British Museum
http://www.thebritishmuseum.ac.uk/world/egypt
Interactive site with sections on daily life, mummification and details of artefacts in the British Museum's collection
http://www.ancientegypt.co.uk

Cleveland Museum of Art (USA)
Includes a young person's site on Egypt.
http://www.clemusart.com/archive/pharaoh/rosetta

Egypt Exploration Society, London
Includes information on current excavations and reports of discoveries in Egypt.
http://www.ees.ac.uk

Griffith Institute, Oxford University
Includes a section on the tomb of Tutankhamun.
http://www.ashmol.ox.ac.uk/Griffith.html

A site aimed at young people.
http://www.geocities.com/young_horus

Egyptology Resources
Probably the most comprehensive site on Egyptology.
http://www.newton.cam.ac.uk/egypt

INDEX

Italic type denotes illustrations

Abu Simbel 66–7, *68*, 89
Abydos 21, 33, 34
Aegean 65, 89, 92
Afghanistan 36, 60
Africa
    circumnavigation of 89
agriculture
    early 8, 9
    Egyptian 12, *12*, 14, *14–15*, *15*, 21, 24, *24*, 25, *25*, 55
Ahmose I 45, 53
Ahmose II 89–90
Akhenaten 30, 59, 60, *60*, 62
Akhetaten 59, 60
Akhmim 35
Akkadian 74
Aleppo 50
Alexander the Great 24, 30, *90*, 91
Alexandria 24, 91, 92–3
Amarna letters archive 59, 60, 61
Amenemhat I 40
Amenemhat II 38, 41
Amenemhat III 36, *36*, 37
Amenhotep I 55
Amenhotep III 59, 60, 65
Amenhotep the son of Hapu 57
amethyst 37, 38
amulets 22, 81
Amun 73, 84, 91
Amun, Temple of, Gebel Barkal 89
Amun, Temple of, Thebes 46, 52, *52*, 64, 68, 69, 80
Anatolia 9, 10, 25, 49, 50, 53, 57, 59, 62, 65, 68, 86, 89, 90, 92
animal cults 85
animal trade 55
Antony 92, 93
Arabia 12
Aramaic 74
architecture 16, *17*, 21–2, 32, 36–7, 58
Armenia 10
artisans *16*, *17*, 21, 52, 76
artistic style 18, 21–3, 34, 55, 60, 73, 80, 85

Ashur-nirari V 77
Ashurnasirpal II *70*, 72
Asia 40–1, 61, 80
Asia, western 8, 9, 12, 19, 24, 25, 53, 55–6, 62, 72, 73, 84, 86, 90, 92
Assyria 9, 53, 57, 59, 65, 72, 74–5, 76, *76*, 77, 78–9, 80, 84, 86
Assyrian army 76, 77, 82
Assyrian Empire 77, 80
    map 83
Aswan 38, 45, 73, 82
Aswan cataract 14
Aswan Dam 12, 14
Asyut 14
Atbara, River 13, *20*
Athens 90
Avaris 42, 44, 45

Babylon 9, 53, 59, 86, 86–7, 90
Babylonia 9, 57, 61, 90
barley 14
'Battlefield Palette' 19
Bayuda Desert 82
Bekaa Valley 63
Bes 40, *40*
Bodhazkoy 65
Book of the Dead 81
bows 50, 60, *70*
bricks 10, 11, 16, 33
Bubastis 80
Buhen 38, 45, 89
building (*see also* architecture)
    Egypt 11, 16, *17*
    Mesopotamia 10, 11
bureaucracy 25, 27, 35, 57–8
burial customs (*see also* mummification, pyramids, tombs) 81, 85
Burton, Richard 93
Buto 24
Byblos 41, 74

Cambyses 90
Canaan 50, *51*, 53, 56, 61, 63
Caria 86, 89, 92
Carthage 74
cartouches 31, *31*, 73
cataracts 14, *20*

cavalry 77
Ceres 89
chariots 48, 49–50, 49, 50, 60, 77
Chatal Huyuk, Turkey 8
Cleopatra VII 92, 93
climate changes 15, 19, 21, 34, 69
coffins 22, 81
colour symbolism 34, 36, 43
copper 10, 12, 18, 37, 61
Crete 44, 61, 65
crocodiles 15, 93
cuneiform script 27, 59
cylinder seals 41
Cyprus 59, 61, 74, 89, 92
Cyrenaica 89
Cyrene 89, 92
Cyrus the Great 90

Damascus 74, 92
Darius I 89
Dashur 33
David, King 73
demotic script 85
Denyen 68
deportation 76, 76, 78–9
deserts 12, 16, 65
diorite 38
diplomacy 57
Dynasty, 3rd
    pyramid building 33
Dynasty, 4th 38
    cartouches 31
    pyramid building 33
    statue 31
Dynasty, 5th pyramid building
    33
Dynasty, 7th 34
Dynasty, 11th 38
Dynasty, 12th 35, 38, 40–2, 44
    architecture 37
Dynasty, 18th 40
    painting 15
    papyrus roll 13
Dynasty, 20th 80, 82
Dynasty, 21st 73
Dynasty, 22nd 80–1

Early Dynastic Period
    pottery lion 21

East Africa 18
ebony 18, 22, 38, 39, 55, 60
education 57
Egypt
    cultural influence 73, 74, 77
Egyptian empire 38, 41, 48–57,
    62–3
Ekwesh 68
elephants 12, 15, 18, 40
Eridu 10
Ethiopia 13, 18, 20, 38, 40
Euphrates 9, 10, 25, 48, 50,
    55, 87

famine 12, 14, 69
Fayum 14
'Fertile Crescent' 9–10, 12
    map 9
First Cataract 14, 16, 18
First Intermediate Period 34
Fourth Cataract 53, 55, 82
furniture 60, 61, 76, 77, 77

Gebel Barkal 89
Gebel Silsila 14
Giza 28, 33, 35, 44
God's Wife of Amun 84, 84
god-kings 15, 31–2
gold 16, 18, 38, 40, 41, 55, 57, 59,
    60, 61, 82
Great Pyramid 33, 35, 44
Greece 61, 65, 89–91, 92

hairstyles 69
Hapy 13
Hatshepsut 30, 40, 54, 56
Hatti 50, 51, 53, 56
Hattusa 65
Hawara 36
Heqa-nefer 59
Herakleopolis 34, 84
Hermopolis 84
Hierakonpolis 18, 20, 21, 22
hieroglyphics 27, 85, 93
hippopotamuses 13, 13, 15, 18
Hittites 10, 49, 50, 53, 57,
    62–3, 65, 73, 74
Horemheb 62
Horn of Africa 40

horses 48, 49–50, 49, 50, 61, 77
Horus 23, 31, 31, 88, 89
Horus amulet 81
houses 16, 44, 58
Hyksos 42, 44, 45, 49, 54
    map 42

ibis 85
Imhotep 32
Inbu-hedji see Memphis
incense 18, 38, 39, 40, 55
Inyotef II, King 35
Ionian coast 86, 89, 92
Iran 77, 86, 90
Iraq (see also Mesopotamia) 9
iron 10, 18
Ishtar Gate 87
Isis 81, 89, 89, 93
    amulet 81
    Roman relief 88
Israel 9, 25, 73, 74, 80
Itjet-tawy 35
ivory 18, 18, 22, 38, 40, 55, 60,
    76, 77

Jehu, King 74–5
Jericho 8
Jerusalem 73, 80, 87, 92
jewellery 18
Jews 87
Jordan, River 74
Judah 73, 74, 80, 84, 87

Kamerernebty, Queen 32
Kamose 45, 53
Karnak 52
Kashta 82
Kassite dynasty 53
Kerma 38, 44, 54
Khafre 30, 31, 31
Khartoum 13, 84
Khonsumose 80
Khufu 31, 33
King's Son of Kush 55
Kiosk of Trajan 92
Knossos 65
Kush 38, 42, 44, 53–5, 58, 72, 73,
    82, 84–5, 89
    glazed tile portrait 55

map 42
    round house pot 44

Lachish 80
lapis lazuli 36, 36, 41, 60–61
Late Bronze Age 50, 53, 59, 69
Late Period sculpture 85, 91, 91
law and women 63
Lebanon 9, 10, 25, 60
Libu tribe 65
Libya 13, 59, 65, 68, 69, 80–1,
    89, 92
Libyan Desert 13
literature 85
Lower Egypt 14, 23, 31, 35
Luxor 65

mace heads 15, 22
Macedonia 72, 91
Maet-hor-neferure 63
Maiherpri 58, 59
Marduk 87
masks 22, 22, 59, 81
Medes 86, 90
Mediterranean 61, 65, 74
Medum 33
Megiddo 49, 56, 87
Memphis 14, 24, 33, 80, 84, 91
Men-nofer see Memphis
Meni (Menes) 24, 31
Menkaure, King 31, 32
Menkheperre-seneb 59
Menthuhotep II, King 34, 35, 35,
    43
Merenptah 65
Meshwesh, Great Chief of the 80
Meshwesh tribe 65, 80
Mesopotamia 8, 9, 10, 24, 25, 53,
    57, 72
    writing 27, 27
metals 10, 16, 18, 61, 74
metalwork 17, 61
Middle Kingdom 30, 35 ff.
    architecture 36–7
    bureaucracy 35, 57
    statues 36, 37, 55
Minoan civilization 42, 44, 61
Mitanni 10, 50, 51, 56, 59–60, 62,
    73, 74

Monthu 45, *45*
mummification 22, 81, 85, 93
mush-hushu 87
Mycenae 61, 65

Nabonidus of Babylon, King 11
Nabopolassar 86
Nanna 11
Napata 89
Naqada 21
Narmer 22–4, *23*
natron 22
Naukratis 89
Neb-kheperu-re *see*
    Tutankhamun
Nebuchadnezzar 87
Nekau II 86–7, 89
Nekhbet 37
Nekhen 18, 34
New Kingdom 30, 48, 49 ff.
    banqueting scene 56
    map *51*
    temples 46, 52, *52*
Nile 12–15
    navigation 14, 33
Nile, Blue 13, *20*, 84
Nile Delta 14, 19, 24, 81, 84, 91
Nile Valley 53
    climate changes 15, 19, 21, 34
    early civilizations 8, 9, 18–19,
        21–2
    flooding 12–14, 15, 21, 24, 31,
        33
    map *20*
Nile, White 13, *20*, 84
Nineveh 86, 90
Nubia 13, 14, 16, 18, 19, *20*, 25,
    35, 37–8, 44, 45, 53–5, 59, 73,
    82, 89

Old Kingdom 30
    boat 33
    bureaucracy 25, 27, 57
    pyramid building 33–4
    statues 33, 37, 55
Orontes, River 12, 56, 63
Osiris 22

Palestine 10, 25, 41, 42, 45, 68, 73,

80, 90
palettes 22–4, *23*
papyri *13, 26, 27, 58, 74, 80, 81,
    93*
Peleset 68
Pepy II, King 34
Persia 72, 89, 90, 91
pharaohs 15, 30, 31–2, 35, 37, *46,*
    52, 54, 55
    Libyan 80–1
Phoenicia 18, 25, 50, *51*, 53, 56,
    68, 74, 89
Piankhy *see* Piye
pictograms 27
Piye 82, 84
Polykrates 90
pottery 8, 18, *19, 21*, 22
Predynastic period 18–19, 21, 22
priestesses 84
priests 21
Psamtik 84–5, 86, 89
Psamtik II 89
Psusennes I
    mask *81*
Ptolemies 91–3
Ptolemy I 91–2
Punt 38, 40
Pyramid of Khafre *28*
pyramids *28,* 30, 32, 33–4, 36, 43,
    44

Qadesh 56, 62, 63
Qadesh, Battle of 49, *49,* 63

Ramesses II 63, 65, 68, 89
Ramesses III 65, 73
Ramesses VI 73
Ramesses XI 73, 82
Red Sea 13, 89
religion 22, 31, 32, 36, 40, 54, 60,
    85, 89, 93
    and women 63, 84
    ceremonies and rituals 15, *15,
    62, 70*
Rome 89, 92–3
royal marriages 57, 59–60

Sais 84, 89
Samaria 73

Samos 90
Sardinia 68
Saul, King 73
scarabs 36, *36*, 81
'Scorpion', King *15*, 22, 24
scribes *26, 27, 57,* 57–8, 93
Sea Peoples 65, *65,* 68–9
Sebekneferu 42
Second Cataract 38, 44, 45,
    53, 73
Senusret I 38
Senusret III 38, *38*
Seqenenre-Tao 45
Sety I 62, 65
Shabaqo 84
Shalmaneser III *74–5*
Shardana 65, 68
Sharuhen 45
Shekelesh 68
Sheshonq I 80
Shuttarna 60
silver 41, 74
Sinai 12, 16, 37, 42
Siwa 91
slaves 55
smith *61*
Solomon, King 73
Somalia 40
Sphinx *28*
'Standard' of Ur *10*
Step Pyramid of Djoser 32, *32,* 33
stone 16, 32, 33, 36, 37, 52
Sudan 13, 14, 38, 40, 55, 82
Sudd 13
Sumerian 27
Syria 9, 10, 25, 48, 49, 50, *51*, 53,
    59, 60, 62, 73, 74, 77, 90

Taharqo 84
Tana, Lake 13
Tanis 63, 73, 80, *81*
Tanis, Temple of 63
Tanwetamani 84
Taweret 40
taxation 25, 27, 55
Taylor, Elizabeth 93
temples 16, 36, 46, *52,* 52, 63, 64,
    66–7, 68, 69, 93
Teresh 68

Thebes 34, 35, 42, 45, 48, 53, 80,
    81, 82, 84, 85
    map *42*
    statues 46
Third Cataract 38
Thoth 85
Thutmose I 55–6, 58
Thutmose III 12, 49, 54, *54*, 55,
    56, 57
Thutmose IV 59
Tiglath-pileser II 77
Tigris 9, 10, 25
timber 9, 10, 16, 49, 60
Tiryns 65
tombs (*see also* pyramids) 8, 16,
    21–2, 33, 34, 43, 81, 85
trade 18, 21, 25, 27, 36, 37–41, 38,
    44, 48, 50, 55, 60–1, 89
Trajan 92
tribute 25, 52, 53, 55
Tunisia 74
turquoise 12, 16, 36, 37
Tutankhamun 36, *50,* 62
    mask *59*
Tyre 74, 83

unification of Egypt 18–19, 21,
    24, 31
Upper Egypt 14, 19, 21, 23, 31, 35
Ur 10, 11, *11*
Ur-Nammu 11

Valley of the Kings 52
Victoria, Lake 13, *20*
viziers 35, 58

Wadi el-Hudi 38
warfare *19,* 34, 38, 45, 48, 49–50,
    53–6, *62,* 62–3, 65, *65,* 68, 76,
    77, 80, 86–7, 89
Wawat 55
wealth 25, 27, 61
Weshesh 68
wheat 14
women 34, 54, 63, 84, 90
writing 8, 26, 27, 50, 59, 74, 84

ziggurats 10, 11, *11*